adorable.
baby knits

25 patterns for boys and girls by Jody Long

Dover Publications, Inc.
Mineola, New York

This book is dedicated to:

My family, for always encouraging me
while I'm under tight deadlines!

Bibliographical Note

Adorable Baby Knits: 25 Patterns for Boys and Girls is a new work, first published by Dover Publications, Inc., in 2016.

International Standard Book Number

ISBN-13: 978-0-486-80739-3
ISBN-10: 0-486-80739-8

Manufactured in the United States by LSC Communications
80739801   2016
www.doverpublications.com

CONTENTS

INTRODUCTION

There is always great joy amongst family and friends when they hear someone is expecting a baby! In this book you will find the perfect garment or accessory to knit for any brand-new bundle of joy or little one celebrating a first birthday, as all the patterns in this book go from newborn to 18 months. With the trends of today, baby showers are becoming the rage and there is nothing more satisfying than receiving a handmade garment knowing that each stitch was made with love and care. The garments range from basic (skill level: one star) to more difficult (skill level: three stars), making this the perfect baby book for all levels of knitters. The main goal of designing this book was to make sure there was plenty of ease in the garments for no-fuss dressing, and most importantly all the yarns are machine washable, making them easy to care for.

Happy knitting!
Jody Long

How to Substitute Yarns

Throughout this book, several different brands and weights of yarn have been used. Always knit a gauge swatch in the new yarn to match the stated gauge in the pattern. It is extremely simple to find a substitute yarn by using this simple equation. If the garment you're going to knit takes seven 3.52oz/100g balls of yarn, which has the yardage of 322/295m, and your new substitute yarn has a yardage of 197/180m, you will need to divide the recommended yarn length total by the new yarn of 197 = balls required. e.g.: 7 x 322yds = 2,254yds needed (recommended). 2,254yds divided by new yarn, which is 197yds, equals 11.44, so you will need twelve 3.52oz/100g balls to complete your garment using the new yarn. I recommend always substituting with the same or similar weight yarn to avoid problems.

Amount of Yarn

Yarn amounts specified in the patterns can never be absolutely correct. This is partly due to the fact that tensions vary according to the knitter, but mostly because the number of yards/meters per ounce/gram varies with every color of yarn. To ensure that you will not run out of yarn, the yarn amounts given in the patterns are generous.

Equipment

Sewing needle: Always use a wool (knitter's) sewing needle for sewing up as these tend to be blunt and will not split the yarn fiber or stitches, resulting in a neater seam.

Stitch holders: These prevent stitches from unravelling when not in use. Alternately, a spare knitting needle of the same size or less (ideally a double pointed) can be used as a stitch holder. For holding just a few stitches, a safety pin is always useful.

Cable needle: There are two types of cable needles: one has a kink and the other is straight, similar to a double-pointed needle. I recommend the one with the kink, as this prevents the stitches from sliding off the needle.

Gauge

It is important to check your tension before you start knitting. Knit a swatch using the specified yarn and knitting needles. If there are too many stitches to 4in/10cm, your tension is tight and you should change to a larger-sized needle. If there are too few stitches, your tension is loose and you should change to a smaller-sized needle.

Casting On (Cable Method)

Although there are many different techniques for casting on stitches, the following method creates a firm and attractive edge:

(1) Make a slip knot in the yarn and place the loop on the left-hand needle. Insert the point of the right-hand needle into the loop on the left-hand needle, wind the yarn round the right-hand needle, and draw the yarn through the loop. Pass the new loop onto the left-hand needle and pull the yarn to tighten the new loop.

(2) Insert the right-hand needle between the two loops on the left-hand needle, wind the yarn around the right-hand needle, and draw the yarn through. Slip the new loop onto the left-hand needle as before.

(3) Continue in this way, inserting the needle between two loops on the left-hand needle, until you have the required number of stitches.

Basic Stitches

Here is how to work the simple stitches used for the garments:

Stockinette Stitch: Alternate one row knit and one row purl. The knit side is the right side of the work unless otherwise stated in the instructions.

Garter Stitch: Knit every row. Both sides are the same and look identical.

K1, P1 Rib: Alternate one knit stitch with one purl stitch to the end of the row. On the next row, knit all the knit stitches and purl all the purl stitches as they face you.

Seed Stitch: Alternate one knit stitch with one purl stitch to the end of the row. On the next row, knit all the purl stitches and purl all the knit stitches as they face you.

Joining Yarn

Always join yarn at the beginning of a new row (unless you're working the Fair Isle or Intarsia Method) and never knot the yarn, as the knot may come through to the right side and spoil your work. Any long loose ends will be useful for sewing up afterwards.

Working Stripes

When knitting different-colored stripes, carry yarns loosely up the side of your work.

Working from a Chart

Each square on a chart represents a stitch and each line of squares a row of knitting. Alongside the chart there will be a color key. When working from the charts, read odd rows (knit) from right to left and even rows (purl) from left to right, unless otherwise stated.

Seams

I recommend mattress stitch, as this helps matching row for row and stripe for stripe on knitted fabric. If you are unable to mattress stitch, then a simple backstitch will be fine. Whichever method you choose for sewing your garment together, a one-stitch seam allowance has been given on all pieces.

Instructions in Parentheses

These are to be repeated the number of times stated after the closing bracket.

Numbers in Brackets

The smallest size is always the first set of numbers just before the opening bracket with the larger sizes inside before the closing of the bracket. Where there is only one number without brackets, this is for all sizes.

Binding Off

Always bind off knit-wise unless otherwise stated.

Working in Stockinette Stitch

Always begin with a K row unless otherwise stated.

US–UK CONVERSION

US	UK
NEEDLE CONVERSION	
0	2.00
1	2.25
–	2.50
2	2.75
2	3.00
3	3.25
4	3.50
5	3.75
6	4.00
7	4.50
8	5.00
9	5.50
10	6.00
10.5	6.50
–	7.00
–	7.50
11	8.00
13	9.00
15	10.00

STITCH CONVERSION

Seed St	Moss St
Stockinette St	Stocking St
Bind off	Cast off
Gauge	Tension

ABBREVIATIONS

alt	alternate
beg	begin/beginning
bet	between
BO	bind off
cm	centimeter(s)
CO	cast on
cont	continue
dec	decrease/decreases/decreasing
dpn	double pointed needle(s)
foll	follow/follows/following
g	gram(s)
Gst	garter stitch
in	inch(es)
inc	increase/increases/increasing
K	knit
Kfb	knit into front and back of next st
k-wise	knit-wise
LHN	left-hand needle
m	marker
mm	millimeter(s)
oz	ounce(s)
P	purl
patt	pattern(s)
pm	place marker
psso	pass slipped stitch over
p-wise	purl-wise
rem	remain/remaining
rep	repeat(s)
Rev St st	reverse stockinette stitch
RHN	right-hand needle
RS	right side
skpo	slip 1, K1, pass slip st over
sl	slip
sl st	slip stitch(es)
St st	stockinette stitch
st(s)	stitch(es)
tbl	through back loop
tog	together
WS	wrong side
y	yarn
yb	yarn to back
yds	yards
yf	yarn to front
yo	yarn over

Baby Banner

Measurements

Skill Level ★

Square Blocks (5.25in/13cm)		
Drops Cotton Light (Off White 01)	2	1.75oz/50g; 115yds/105m
Drops Cotton Light (Light Pink 05)	1	1.75oz/50g; 115yds/105m
Drops Cotton Light (Ice Blue 08)	1	1.75oz/50g; 115yds/105m

Materials

* 1 Pair US 3 (3.25mm) knitting needles OR SIZE TO OBTAIN GAUGE
* 1 Small safety pin
* 2.2yds (2m) of narrow ribbon

Gauge

25 sts and 36 rows = 4in/10cm in St st. TAKE TIME TO CHECK GAUGE.

BLOCKS

(Make 2 B's, 1 A, and 1 Y in Off White; 3 Light Pink hearts and 2 Ice Blue hearts)
CO 33.

Rows 1–49 Follow charts, ending with WS row.
BO knitwise.

FINISHING

Weave in ends. Block squares to measurements. Use a safety pin to thread ribbon through blocks as illustrated above.

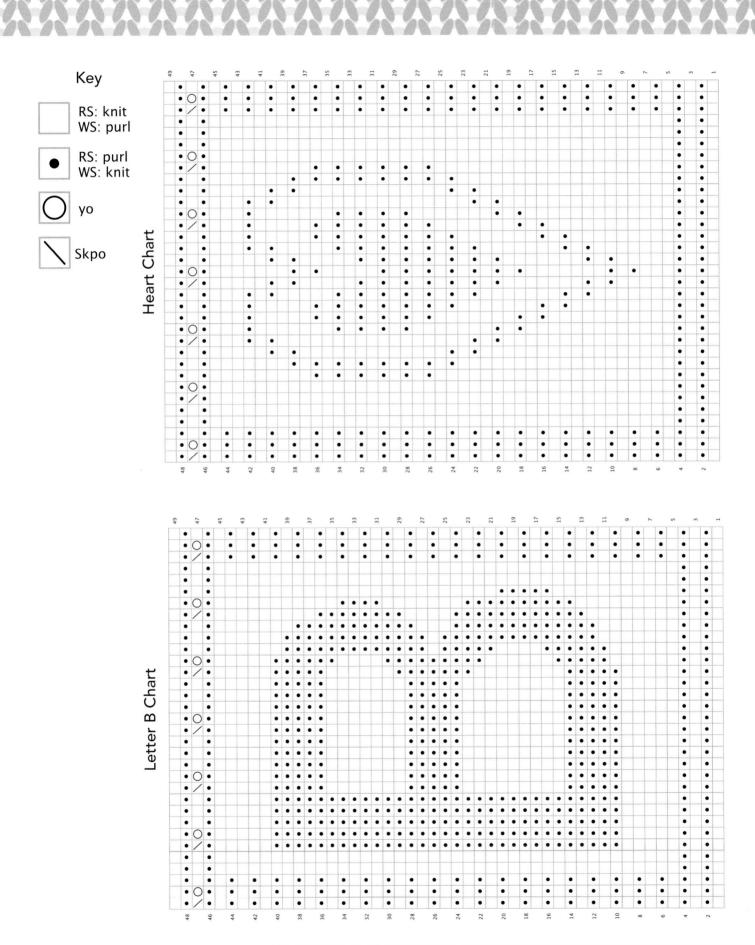

Key

RS: knit
WS: purl

RS: purl
WS: knit

yo

Skpo

Heart Chart

Letter B Chart

Letter A Chart

Letter Y Chart

Fisherman's Rib Booties

Measurements

Skill Level ★

Size	0–3 months	3–6 months	
Red Heart Lisa (Baby Blue 5665)	1	1	1.75oz/50g; 145yds/133m

Materials

* 1 Pair US 6 (4mm) knitting needles OR SIZE TO OBTAIN GAUGE

Gauge

22 sts and 28 rows = 4in/10cm in St st. TAKE TIME TO CHECK GAUGE.

SPECIAL ABBREVIATIONS

K1B Insert needle into next stitch one row below.

1/1 Rib (over an odd number of sts) **Row 1** K1, [P1, K1] across. **Row 2** P1, [K1, P1] across. Rep Rows 1–2.

Skpo Slip next st from LHN to RHN as if to knit, without knitting it. K next st and slip the slipped st over this last K st. (1 st decreased)

S2kpo Slip next 2 sts from LHN to RHN as if to K2tog, without knitting them. K next st and slip the 2 slipped sts over this last K st. (2 sts decreased)

BOOTIES (make 2)

CUFF

CO 31 (33).

Row 1 (RS) Knit.

Row 2 P1, [K1B, P1] across.

Rows 3–14 Rep Rows 1–2.

Rows 15–22 Work 1/1 Rib.

Rows 23–26 (28) Work even in St st.

SHAPE INSTEP

Row 27 (29) K21 (22) turn.

Row 28 (30) P11, turn.

Rows 29–36 (31–40) Work even in St st on 11 sts only.

Row 37 (41) K1, skpo, K to last 3 sts, K2tog, K1 — 9 sts.

Row 38 (42) Purl.

Rows 39–40 (43–44) Rep the last 2 rows — 7 sts. Cut yarn.

FOOT

Row 41 (45) With RS facing, join yarn to inner edge of first 10 (11) sts, pick up and K8 (10) sts evenly along right side of instep, K across 7 sts of toe, pick up and K8 (10) sts evenly along left side of instep and K across rem 10 (11) sts — 43 (49) sts.

Rows 42–46 (46–50) G st.

SHAPE FOOT

Row 47 (51) (RS) K1, skpo, K14 (17), K2tog, K5, skpo, K14 (17), K2tog, K1 — 39 (45) sts.

Row 48 (52) And all foll WS rows Knit.

Row 49 (53) K1, skpo, K13 (16), K2tog, K3, skpo, K13 (16), K2tog, K1 — 35 (41) sts.

Row 51 (55) K1, skpo, K12 (15), K2tog, K1, skpo, K12 (15), K2tog, K1 — 31 (37) sts.

Row 53 (57) K1, skpo, K11 (14), s2kpo, K11 (14), K2tog, K1 — 27 (33) sts.

Row 54 (58) Knit. BO leaving tail for finishing.

FINISHING

Fold BO edge and sew to close sole, continue up heel, joining ends of rows 26 (28) –1, reversing seam for cuff.

Seed Stitch Booties

Measurements

Skill Level ★

Size	0–3 months	3–6 months	
Sirdar Snuggly DK (Pink 212)	1	1	1.75oz/50g; 179yds/164m

Materials

* 1 Pair US 6 (4mm) knitting needles OR SIZE TO OBTAIN GAUGE

Gauge

22 sts and 28 rows = 4in/10cm in St st. TAKE TIME TO CHECK GAUGE.

BOOTIES (make 2)

CUFF

CO 31 (33) sts.

Rows 1–17 (19) K1, [P1, K1] across.

Rows 18 (20)–22 (26) St st.

INSTEP

Row 23 (27) K21 (22) turn.

Row 24 (28) P11, turn.

Rows 25 (29)–32 (38) Work even in St st on 11 sts only.

Row 33 (39) (RS) K1, skpo, K to last 3 sts, K2tog, K1 — 9 sts.

Row 34 (40) Purl.

Rows 35–36 (41–42) Rep the last 2 rows — 7 sts. Cut yarn.

FOOT

Row 37 (43) With RS facing, join yarn to inner edge of first 10 (11) sts, pick up and K8 (10) sts evenly along right side of instep, K across 7 sts of toe, pick up and K8 (10) sts evenly along left side of instep and K across rem 10 (11) sts — 43 (49) sts.

Rows 38–42 (44–48) G st.

SHAPE FOOT

Row 43 (49) (RS) K1, skpo, K14 (17), K2tog, K5, skpo, K14 (17), K2tog, K1 — 39 (45) sts.

Row 44 (50) and all foll WS rows Knit.

Row 45 (51) K1, skpo, K13 (16), K2tog, K3, skpo, K13 (16), K2tog, K1 — 35 (41) sts.

Row 47 (53) K1, skpo, K12 (15), K2tog, K1, skpo, K12 (15), K2tog, K1 — 31 (37) sts.

Row 49 (55) K1, skpo, K11 (14), s2kpo, K11 (14), K2tog, K1 — 27 (33) sts.

Row 50 (56) Knit. BO leaving tail for finishing.

FINISHING

Fold BO edge and sew to close sole, continue up heel, joining ends of rows 26 (28)–1, reversing seam for cuff.

Rainbow Booties

Measurements

Size	0–3 months	3–6 months	
Lion Brand Modern Baby (Blue 109)	1	1	2.6oz/75g; 172yds/158m
Lion Brand Modern Baby (Red 113)	1	1	2.6oz/75g; 172yds/158m
Lion Brand Modern Baby (Orange 133)	1	1	2.6oz/75g; 172yds/158m
Lion Brand Modern Baby (Yellow 158)	1	1	2.6oz/75g; 172yds/158m
Lion Brand Modern Baby (Green 130)	1	1	2.6oz/75g; 172yds/158m

Materials

* 1 Pair US 6 (4mm) knitting needles OR SIZE TO OBTAIN GAUGE

Gauge

22 sts and 28 rows = 4in/10cm in St st. TAKE TIME TO CHECK GAUGE.

SPECIAL ABBREVIATIONS

1/1 Rib (over an odd number of sts) **Row 1** K1, [P1, K1] across. **Row 2** P1, [K1, P1] across. Rep Rows 1–2.

BOOTIES (make 2)

CUFF

With Blue, CO 31 (33) sts.

Rows 1–18 Work 1/1 Rib.

Rows 19–22 (24) Work even in St st.

SHAPE INSTEP

Row 23 (25) K21 (22) turn.

Row 24 (26) P11, turn.

Rows 25–32 (27–34) Cont working even in St st on 11 sts only in the foll stripe pattern.

2 rows each in Red, Orange, Yellow, and Green.

0–3 MONTHS ONLY

Row 33 With Blue, K1, skpo, K to last 3 sts, K2tog, K1 — 9 sts.

Row 34 Purl.

Row 35 With Red, K1, skpo, K to last 3 sts, K2tog, K1 — 7 sts.

Row 36 Purl. Cut yarn.

3–6 MONTHS ONLY

Rows 35–36 With Blue, work even in St st.

Row 37 With Red, K1, skpo, K to last 3 sts, K2tog, K1 — 9 sts.

Row 38 Purl.

Row 39 With Orange, K1, skpo, K to last 3 sts, K2tog, K1 — 7 sts.

Row 40 Purl. Cut yarn.

BOTH SIZES (Cont with Blue for remainder of bootie)

FOOT

Row 37 (41) With RS facing, join yarn to inner edge of first 10 (11) sts, pick up and K8 (10) sts evenly along right side of instep, K across 7 sts of toe, pick up and K8 (10) sts evenly along left side of instep and K across rem 10 (11) sts — 43 (49) sts.

Rows 38–42 (42–46) G st.

SHAPE FOOT

Row 43 (47) (RS) K1, skpo, K14 (17), K2tog, K5, skpo, K14 (17), K2tog, K1 — 39 (45) sts.

Row 44 (48) and all foll WS rows Knit.

Row 45 (49) K1, skpo, K13 (16), K2tog, K3, skpo, K13 (16), K2tog, K1 — 35 (41) sts.

Row 47 (51) K1, skpo, K12 (15), K2tog, K1, skpo, K12 (15), K2tog, K1 — 31 (37) sts.

Row 49 (53) K1, skpo, K11 (14), s2kpo, K11 (14), K2tog, K1 — 27 (33) sts.

Row 50 (54) Knit. BO leaving tail for finishing.

FINISHING

Fold BO edge and sew to close sole, continue up heel, joining ends of rows 26 (28)–1, reversing seam for cuff.

Rainbow Hat

Measurements

Skill Level ★

Size	0–3 months	3–6 months	6–12 months	12–18 months	
Lion Brand Modern Baby (Blue 109)	1	1	1	1	2.6oz/75g; 172yds/158m
Lion Brand Modern Baby (Red 113)	1	1	1	1	2.6oz/75g; 172yds/158m
Lion Brand Modern Baby (Orange 133)	1	1	1	1	2.6oz/75g; 172yds/158m
Lion Brand Modern Baby (Yellow 158)	1	1	1	1	2.6oz/75g; 172yds/158m
Lion Brand Modern Baby (Green 130)	1	1	1	1	2.6oz/75g; 172yds/158m

Materials

* 1 Pair US 3 (3.25mm) knitting needles
* 1 Pair US 6 (4mm) knitting needles OR SIZE TO OBTAIN GAUGE

Gauge

22 sts and 28 rows = 4in/10cm in St st with larger needles. TAKE TIME TO CHECK GAUGE.

SPECIAL ABBREVIATIONS

1/1 Rib (over an odd number of sts) **Row 1** K1, [P1, K1] across. **Row 2** P1, [K1, P1] across. Rep Rows 1–2.

STRIPE PATTERN

Beg with a K row, work 4 rows even in St st in the foll stripe pattern:

Red, Orange, Yellow, Green, Blue.

HAT

With smaller needles and Blue, CO 71 (81, 81, 91).

Rows 1–19 (21, 21, 23) Work 1/1 Rib.

Change to larger needles and work even in stripe patt until hat measures 6 (6.5, 6.75, 7.25)in/15 (16.5, 17, 18)cm from beg.

SHAPE CROWN (maintaining stripe pattern)

Row 1 (RS) K1, [K2tog, K3] across — 57 (65, 65, 73) sts.

Row 2 and all WS rows Purl.

Row 3 K1, [K2tog, K2] across — 43 (49, 49, 55) sts.

Row 5 K1, [K2tog, K1] across — 29 (33, 33, 37) sts.

Row 7 K1, K2tog across — 15 (17, 17, 19) sts.

Row 8 P1, P2tog across — 8 (9, 9, 10) sts.

Cut yarn leaving a tail, thread tail through rem sts, pull up tightly and fasten off.

FINISHING

Sew row ends tog, matching stripes and reversing seam halfway into rib section.

Flower Picot Hat

Measurements

Skill Level ★

Size	0–6 months	6–12 months	12–18 months	
Red Heart Lisa DK (Fire 207)	1	1	1	1.75oz/50g; 145yds/133m
Red Heart Lisa DK (Candy 8305)	1	1	1	1.75oz/50g; 145yds/133m

Materials

* 1 Pair US 3 (3.25mm) knitting needles
* 1 Pair US 5 (3.75mm) knitting needles
* 1 Pair US 6 (4mm) knitting needles **OR SIZE TO OBTAIN GAUGE.**

Gauge

22 sts and 30 rows = 4in/10cm in St st using largest needles. TAKE TIME TO CHECK GAUGE.

HAT

Using US 5 (3.75mm) needles and Fire, CO 75 (79, 83) sts.

Rows 1–3, 5–6 St st.

Row 4 Picot row (WS) K1, [yo, K2tog] across.

Rows 7–10 G st.

Change to US 6 (4mm) needles and Candy.

Work even in St st until hat measures 3.75 (4, 4.5)in/9.5 (10, 11)cm from picot row.

Next row (WS) P, dec 4 (dec 1, inc 2) sts evenly spaced across — 71 (78, 85) sts.

SHAPE CROWN

Row 1 (RS) [K5, K2tog] across to last st, K1 — 61 (67, 73) sts.

Rows 2–4, 6–8 St st.

Row 5 [K4, K2tog] across to last st, K1 — 51 (56, 61) sts.

Row 9 [K3, K2tog] across to last st, K1 — 41 (45, 49) sts.

Rows 10, 12, 14 Purl.

Row 11 [K2, K2tog] across to last st, K1 — 31 (34, 37) sts.

Row 13 [K1, K2tog] across to last st, K1 — 21 (23, 25) sts.

Row 15 K2tog across to last st, K1 — 11 (12, 13) sts.

Row 16 (WS) P1 (0, 1), P2tog across — 6 (6, 7) sts.

Cut yarn leaving a tail, thread tail through rem sts, pull up tightly and fasten off securely.

FLOWERS (Make 3)

Using US 3 (3.25mm) needles and Fire, CO 25 sts.

Rows 1–3 St st.

Row 4 Picot row (WS) K1, [yo, K2tog] across.

Rows 5–6 St st. BO purlwise.

FINISHING

Sew ends of rows forming a seam down center back. Fold hem on picot row to wrong side and slip stitch in place.

Fold CO and BO edges of each flower together with RS outside and slip stitch together. Roll the strip up tightly lengthways to form a flower shape, work several stitches into base of each flower to hold shape. Sew the flowers in a cluster as illustrated, with seam on hat at center back.

Frilly Sun Hat

Measurements   **Skill Level ★**

Size	0–3 months	3–6 months	6–12 months	12–18 months	
Debbie Bliss Eco Baby Prints (Blossom 008)	2	2	2	3	1.75oz/50g; 136yds/124m

Materials

* 1 US 3 (3.25mm) 32in/80cm circular needle OR SIZE TO OBTAIN GAUGE

Gauge

25 sts and 34 rows = 4in/10cm in St st. TAKE TIME TO CHECK GAUGE.

HAT

CO 86 (92, 98, 104) sts.

Work back and forth in St st until hat measures 3.75 (4, 4.25, 4.75)in/9.5 (10, 11, 12)cm.

SHAPE CROWN

Row 1 (RS) K3 (1, 4, 3), [K2tog, K7] across to last 2 (1, 4, 2) sts, K2 (1, 4, 2) — 77 (82, 88, 93) sts.

Rows 2–4 St st.

Row 5 K3 (1, 0, 3), [K2tog, K6] across to last 2 (1, 4, 2) sts, K2 (1, 0, 2) — 68 (72, 77, 82) sts.

Rows 6, 8, 10, 12, 14 Purl.

Row 7 K3 (1, 0, 3), [K2tog, K5] across to last 2 (1, 0, 2) sts, K2 (1, 0, 2) — 59 (62, 66, 71) sts.

Row 9 K3 (1, 0, 3), [K2tog, K4] across to last 2 (1, 0, 2) sts, K2 (1, 0, 2) — 50 (52, 55, 60) sts.

Row 11 K0 (1, 0, 0), [K2tog, K3] across to last 0 (1, 0, 0) sts, K0 (1, 0, 0) — 40 (42, 44, 48) sts.

Row 13 K0 (1, 0, 0), [K2tog, K2] across to last 0 (1, 0, 0) sts, K0 (1, 0, 0) — 30 (32, 33, 36) sts.

Row 15 K0 (1, 0, 0), [K2tog, K1] across to last 0 (1, 0, 0) sts, K0 (1, 0, 0) — 20 (22, 22, 24) sts.

Row 16 P2tog 10 (11, 11, 12) times — 10 (11, 11, 12) sts.

Cut yarn leaving a long tail, thread tail through rem sts, pull up tightly and fasten off.

FRILL

Row 1 With RS facing and circular needle, pick up and K86 (92, 98, 104) sts along cast on edge.

Rows 2–4 Work back and forth in G st.

Row 5 K1, [m1, K1, m1, K2] across to last st, K1 — 142 (152, 162, 172) sts.

Rows 6, 8 Knit.

Row 7 K1, [m1, K3, m1, K2] across to last st, K1 — 198 (212, 226, 240) sts.

Row 9 K1, [m1, K5, m1, K2] across to last st, K1 — 254 (272, 290, 308) sts.

Rows 10–15 (17, 19, 21) G st.

Picot bind off row (WS) BO 2 sts, [place st from right hand needle back onto left hand needle, CO 2 sts, BO 4 sts] across. Fasten off.

Teddy Bear Blanket

Measurements   Skill Level ★

For Blanket	13in/33cm	
Patons Fairytale Cloud (Pastel Blue 52)	2	0.9oz/25g; 90yds/82m
For Teddy Bear Head (approximately)	3in/7.5cm	
Patons Fab DK (Beige 2331)	1	3.5oz/100g; 300yds/274m

Materials

* 1 Pair US 2 (2.75mm) knitting needles OR SIZE TO OBTAIN GAUGE
* 1 Pair US 6 (4mm) knitting needles OR SIZE TO OBTAIN GAUGE
* Stitch marker
* Small amount of black DK weight yarn
* Small amount of toy stuffing

Gauge

20 sts and 36 rows = 4in/10cm in G st using larger needles and Patons Fairytale Cloud.

25 sts and 36 rows = 4in/10cm in St st using smaller needles and Patons Fab DK.

TAKE TIME TO CHECK GAUGE.

BLANKET

Using larger needles and Pastel Blue, loosely CO 68.

Work even in G st until work measures 13in/33cm from beg, ending with a WS row.

BO loosely, weave in ends.

BEAR

HEAD

Using smaller needles and Beige, CO 10.

Rows 1–2 St st.

Row 3 Kfb in each st across — 20 sts.

Row 4 and foll WS rows Purl.

Row 5 [Kfb, K1] across — 30 sts.

Row 7 [K1, Kfb, K1] across — 40 sts.

Row 9 [K1, Kfb, K2] across — 50 sts.

Rows 10–20 St st.

SHAPE TOP OF HEAD

Row 21 [K1, K2tog, K2] across — 40 sts.

Row 22 and foll WS rows Purl.

Row 23 [K1, K2tog, K1] across — 30 sts.

Row 25 [K1, K2tog] across — 20 sts.

Row 27 K2tog across — 10 sts.

Cut yarn leaving a tail, thread tail through rem sts, pull up tightly and fasten off. Sew row ends of head tog leaving a small gap. Stuff firmly and close gap. With seam running down center back, sew base edge of head to center of blanket.

MUZZLE

Using smaller needles and Beige, CO 28 sts.

Rows 1–4 G st.

Row 5 [K1, K2tog, K1] across — 21 sts.

Row 6 Knit.

Row 7 [K1, K2tog] across — 14 sts.

BO knitwise, pm at center.

Sew row ends together. Match seam with marker and sew across the BO edges tog.

Stuff firmly and sew to front of head as illustrated.

EARS (make 2)

Using smaller needles and Beige, CO 10.

Rows 1–6 St st, BO.

With RS out sew CO and BO edges tog. Fold in half with row ends at base of ear, sew to top of head as illustrated.

ARMS (make 2)

Using smaller needles and Beige, CO 14.

Rows 1–24 St st.

Row 25 (RS) K2tog across — 7 sts.

Cut yarn leaving a tail, thread tail through rem sts, pull up tightly and fasten off. Sew row ends tog leaving CO edge open. Stuff lightly, sew CO edges of each arm to either side of head with seams facing toward the back. Sew ends of hands tog and pull a small section of blanket into arms as illustrated.

Facial Features

Using a length of Black yarn, embroider eyes using straight stitches 5 rows high with 4 sts bet. Work over the first line to widen each eye as illustrated. Using another length of Black yarn, work several straight sts for the nose on the muzzle as illustrated, gradually working into a point. Embroider a vertical line from center bottom of nose and 2 tiny straight stitches for the mouth as illustrated.

Rosette Blanket

Measurements **Skill Level ★**

Blanket (excluding border)	29 x 26 in/ 74 x 66 cm	
Cascade Cherub DK (Ecru 09)	8	1.75oz/50g; 180yds/165m

Materials

* 1 Pair US 3 (3.25mm) knitting needles
* 1 Pair US 6 (4mm) knitting needles OR SIZE TO OBTAIN GAUGE

Gauge

23 sts and 30 rows = 4in/10cm in St st using larger needles. TAKE TIME TO CHECK GAUGE.

SPECIAL ABBREVIATIONS

S2kpo Slip next 2 sts from LHN to RHN as if to K2tog, without knitting them, K next st and slip the 2 slipped sts over this last K st — 2 sts decreased.

BLANKET

Using larger needles, CO 137.

Rows 1–4 Knit.

Row 5 Knit.

Row 6 K2, [P25, K2] across.

Rows 7–28 Rep rows 5–6.

Rows 29–32 Knit.

Rep Rows 5–32 6 times. BO, weave in ends.

ROSES (Make 18)

Using smaller needles, CO 25.

Rows 1–3 St st.

Row 4 Picot row (WS) K1, [yo, K2tog] across.

Rows 5–7 St st. BO purlwise.

FINISHING

Sew CO and BO edges together with RS outside. Roll strip tightly to form a flower, with picot row facing upward to form petals. Sew base of each flower to secure shape. Sew one flower in the center of alternating squares as illustrated.

LEAVES (Make 36)

Using smaller needles, CO 3 sts.

Row 1 (RS) K1, [m1, K1] 2 times — 5 sts.

Row 2 and all WS rows Knit.

Row 3 K2, m1, K1, m1, K2 — 7 sts.

Row 5 K3, m1, K1, m1, K3 — 9 sts.

Row 7 Knit.

Row 9 Skpo, K to last 2 sts, K2tog — 7 sts.

Row 10 Knit.

Rows 11–14 Rep last 2 rows twice — 3 sts

Row 15 K3tog, Fasten off.

FINISHING

Sew the CO edge of a leaf at each side of each rose as illustrated.

BORDER

Using smaller needles, CO 6 sts.

Row 1 (RS) K3, yo, K1, yo, K2 — 8 sts.

Row 2 P6, Kfb, K1 — 9 sts.

Row 3 K2, P1, K2, yo, K1, yo, K3 — 11 sts.

Row 4 P8, Kfb, K2 — 12 sts.

Row 5 K2, P2, K3, yo, K1, yo, K4 — 14 sts.

Row 6 P10, Kfb, K3 — 15 sts.

Row 7 K2, P3, skpo, K5, K2tog, K1 — 13 sts.

Row 8 P8, Kfb, P1, K3 — 14 sts.

Row 9 K2, P1, K1, P2, skpo, K3, K2tog, K1 — 12 sts.

Row 10 P6, Kfb, K1, P1, K3 — 13 sts.

Row 11 K2, P1, K1, P3, skpo, K1, K2tog, K1 — 11 sts.

Row 12 P4, Kfb, K2, P1, K3 — 12 sts.

Row 13 K2, P1, K1, P4, s2kpo, K1 — 10 sts.

Row 14 P2tog, BO 3, K1, P1, K3 — 6 sts.

Rep Rows 1–14 for patt.

Sew straight edge of border to edge of blanket as you go, starting from bottom right corner. Ending with row 14, BO. Sew CO edge of border to BO edge of border.

Easy Henley

Measurements Skill Level ★

Size	0–3 months	3–6 months	6–12 months	12–18 months	
To Fit Chest	16 41	18 46	20 51	22 56	in cm
Actual Size	17.5 44	20 51	22 56	24.5 62	in cm
Full Length (approximately)	8.5 21.5	10 25.5	11.5 29	13 33	in cm
Sleeve Length (adjustable)	6 15	6.5 16.5	7.5 19	8.5 21.5	in cm
Sirdar Snuggly Baby Crofter DK (Scottie 152)* *Please note the color pattern of sweater as shown in photos is due to the nature of the yarn suggested here.	2	2	3	3	1.75oz/ 50g; 179yds/ 164m

Materials

* 1 Pair US 3 (3.25mm) knitting needles
* 1 Pair US 6 (4mm) knitting needles OR SIZE TO OBTAIN GAUGE
* Stitch markers
* Stitch holders
* 2 Buttons
* Sewing needle and thread

Gauge

22 sts and 30 rows = 4in/10cm in St st with larger needles. TAKE TIME TO CHECK GAUGE.

SWEATER

BACK

With smaller needles, CO 50 (56, 62, 68) sts.

Rows 1–6 G st.

Row 7 (RS) Change to larger needles, Knit.

Row 8 K4, *P to last 4 sts, K4.

Rows 9–16 (18, 20, 22) Rep last 2 rows.

Place markers in st at each end of last row to mark side edge openings.

Rows 17–64 (19–76, 21–86, 23–98) Work even in St st or until back measures 8.5 (10, 11.5, 13)in/21.5 (25.5, 29, 33)cm, ending with WS row.

SHAPE SHOULDERS

Rows 65–68 (77–80, 87–90, 99–102) BO 5 (6, 7, 7) sts at beg of row — 30 (32, 34, 40) sts.

Rows 69–70 (81–82, 91–92, 103–104) BO 6 (6, 6, 8) sts at beg of — 18 (20, 22, 24) sts.

Place rem 18 (20, 22, 24) sts on holder.

FRONT

Work as for back to Row 36 (48, 56, 68) or until front measures 4.75 (6.25, 7.5, 9) in/12 (16, 19, 23)cm, ending with WS row.

DIVIDE FOR FRONT OPENING

Row 37 (49, 57, 69) (RS) K27 (30, 33, 36), turn, leaving rem sts unworked.

Row 38 (50, 58, 70) K4, P across.

Row 39 (51, 59, 71) Knit.

Rows 40–46 (52–58, 60–66, 72–78) Rep last 2 rows.

Row 47 (59, 67, 79) Buttonhole row (RS) K to last 3 sts, yo, K2tog, K1.

Rows 48–50 (60–62, 68–70, 80–82) Work even in patt as established.

SHAPE NECK

Row 51 (63, 71, 83) (RS) K22 (24, 27, 29), turn, place 5 (6, 6, 7) sts on holder.

Rows 52–55 (64–67, 72–75, 84–87) Cont in St st, dec 1 st at neck edge — 18 (20, 23, 25) sts.

Row 56 (68, 76, 88) Work even in St st..

Row 57 (69, 77, 89) Cont in St st, dec 1 st at neck edge – 17 (19, 22, 24) sts.

Rows 58–59 (70–71, 78–81, 90–93) Rep last 2 rows — 16 (18, 20, 22) sts.

Rows 60–64 (72–76, 82–86, 94–98) Work even in St st.

SHAPE SHOULDER

Row 65 (77, 87, 99) BO 5 (6, 7, 7) sts beg of row — 11 (12, 13, 15) sts.

Row 66 (78, 88, 100) Work even in St st.

Rows 67–68 (79–80, 89–90, 101–102) Rep last 2 rows — 6 (6, 6, 8) sts.

Row 69 (81, 91, 103) BO.

SECOND SIDE

Row 37 (49, 57, 69) (RS) CO 4 sts, with RS facing, K across rem sts — 27 (30, 33, 36) sts.

Row 38 (50, 58, 70) P to last 4 sts, K4.

Row 39 (51, 59, 71) Knit.

Rows 40–50 (52–62, 60–70, 72–82) Rep last 2 rows.

SHAPE NECK AND SHOULDER

Complete to match first side, reversing shaping.

SLEEVES (Make 2)

With smaller needles, CO 28 (30, 32, 34).

Rows 1–6 G st.

Row 7 (RS) Change to larger needles, Knit.

Cont in St st, inc as foll:

Inc 1 st on each end of 3rd (3rd, 5th, 5th) row — 30 (32, 34, 36) sts.

Inc 1 st on each end of every 4th row 1 (4, 6, 6) times — 32 (40, 46, 48) sts.

Inc 1 st on each end of every 4th (4th, 6th, 6th) row 6 (4, 3, 2) times — 44 (48, 52, 56) sts.

Work even until sleeve measures 6 (6.5, 7.5, 8.5)in/15 (16.5, 19, 21.5)cm, ending with WS row.

SHAPE CAP

BO 3 (3, 4, 4) sts at beg of next 4 rows.

BO 5 (6, 6, 7) sts at beg of next 4 rows.

BO rem 12 sts.

NECKBAND

Sew shoulder seams.

Row 1 (RS) With RS facing and smaller needles, move 5 (6, 6, 7) sts from right front st holder to RH needle, join yarn and pick up and K14 (14, 16, 16) sts on right side of neck, K18 (20, 22, 24) sts from back st holder, pick up and K14 (14, 16, 16) sts on left side of neck, K 5 (6, 6, 7) sts from left front st holder — 56 (60, 66, 70) sts.

Rows 2–4 G st.

Row 5 Buttonhole row (RS) K to last 3 sts, yo, K2tog, K1.

Rows 6–7 G st.

Row 8 BO knitwise.

FINISHING

Place markers on front and back 4.75 (5.25, 5.5, 5.75)in/12 (13, 14, 15)cm down from shoulder seams. Sew sleeves centered on shoulder seams bet markers. Sew side and sleeve seams, leaving side seams open below marker. At neck opening, sew cast on edge of right front behind left front border. Sew on buttons to correspond with buttonholes.

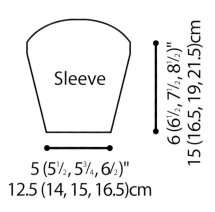

Sleeve

6 (6½, 7½, 8½)"
15 (16.5, 19, 21.5)cm

5 (5½, 5¾, 6½)"
12.5 (14, 15, 16.5)cm

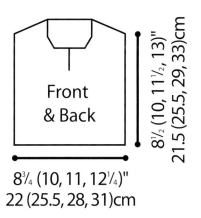

Front & Back

8½ (10, 11½, 13)"
21.5 (25.5, 29, 33)cm

8¾ (10, 11, 12¼)"
22 (25.5, 28, 31)cm

Sheep Sweater

Measurements

Skill Level ★ ★

Size	0–3 months	3–6 months	6–12 months	12–18 months	
To Fit Chest	16 41	18 46	20 51	22 56	in cm
Actual Size	18.5 47	20.5 52	22.5 57	24.5 62	in cm
Full Length (approximately)	9.5 24	11 28	12.5 32	14 35.5	in cm
Sleeve Length (adjustable)	6 15	6.5 16.5	7.5 19	8.5 21.5	in cm
Cascade Cherub DK (Grass 21)	2	2	3	4	1.75oz/50g; 180yds/165m
Cascade Cherub DK (Ecru 09)	1	1	1	1	1.75oz/50g; 180yds/165m
Cascade Cherub DK (Black 40)	1	1	1	1	1.75oz/50g; 180yds/165m

Materials

* 1 Pair US 3 (3.25mm) knitting needles
* 1 Pair US 6 (4mm) knitting needles OR SIZE TO OBTAIN GAUGE
* Stitch holders
* Stitch markers
* 1 Button
* 2 Snaps
* Sewing needle and thread

Gauge

23 sts and 30 rows = 4in/10cm in St st with larger needles. TAKE TIME TO CHECK GAUGE.

SWEATER

BACK

With smaller needles and Grass, CO 54 (60, 66, 72) sts.

Rows 1–6 G st.

Change to larger needles, work even in St st until back measures 6.25 (8, 9.5, 11) in/16 (20, 24, 28)cm, ending with WS row.

DIVIDE FOR BACK OPENING

First Side

Next row (RS) K29 (32, 35, 38), turn, leaving rem sts unworked.

Next row K4, P across.

Next row Knit.

Rep last 2 rows until back opening measures 2.75in/7cm, ending with WS row.

Shape Shoulder

Maintaining border sts, BO 6 (6, 7, 8) sts at beg of next 2 RS rows.

BO 5 (7, 7, 7) sts at beg of next row (neck edge).

Work 1 row even, place rem 12 (13, 14, 15) sts on holder.

Second Side

With RS facing, join yarn, CO 4 sts, K across — 29 (32, 35, 38) sts.

Next row (WS) P to last 4 sts, K4.

Next row Knit.

Rep last 2 rows until back opening measures 2.75in/7cm, ending with RS row.

Shape Shoulder

Maintaining border sts, BO 6 (6, 7, 8) sts at beg of next 2 WS rows.

BO 5 (7, 7, 7) sts at beg of next row (neck edge), place rem 12 (13, 14, 15) sts on holder.

FRONT

With smaller needles and Grass, CO 54 (60, 66, 72) sts.

Rows 1–6 G st.

Rows 7–18 (28, 34, 40) Change to larger needles, St st.

Note Using Intarsia method and a separate yarn for each block of color, twist yarns tog on WS at color change to avoid holes.

Row 19 (29, 35, 41) (RS) K10 (13, 16, 19), pm, work chart over next 34 sts, pm, K10 (13, 16, 19).

Row 20 (30, 36, 42) (WS), P10 (13, 16, 19), work chart bet markers, P10 (13, 16, 19).

Sheep Chart

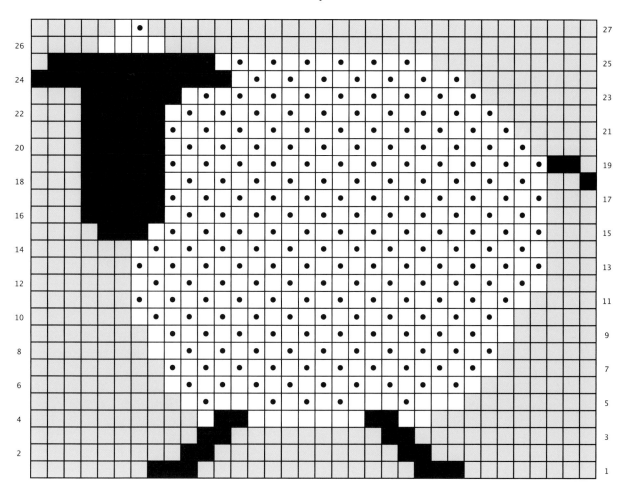

Key

□	RS: knit WS: purl
☐•	RS: purl WS: knit
▨	Grass
□	Ecru
■	Black

Rows 21–45 (31–55, 37–61, 43–67) Rep last 2 rows to work chart.

With Grass, work even in St st until work measures 7.25 (8.75, 10, 11.75) in/18 (22, 25.5, 30)cm or 14 (14, 16, 16) rows less than back at start of shoulder shaping, ending with WS row.

SHAPE NECK

First Side

Next row (RS) K23 (25, 28, 30), turn, leaving rem sts unworked.

Dec 1 st at neck edge on next 4 rows.

Dec 1 st at neck edge on next 2 (2, 3, 3) RS rows — 17 (19, 21, 23) sts.

Work 5 rows in St st, ending with a WS row.

Shape Shoulder

BO 6 (6, 7, 8) sts at beg of next 2 RS rows.

P 1 row, BO rem 5 (7, 7, 7) sts.

Second Side

With RS facing, place 8 (10, 10, 12) sts on holder, join yarn, K across — K23 (25, 28, 30) sts.

Dec 1 st at neck edge on next 4 rows.

Dec 1 st at neck edge on next 2 (2, 3, 3) RS rows — 17 (19, 21, 23) sts.

Work 6 rows in St st.

Shape Shoulder

BO 6 (6, 7, 8) sts at beg of next 2 RS rows.

K 1 row, BO rem 5 (7, 7, 7) sts.

SLEEVES (Make 2)

With Smaller needles and Grass, CO 32 (34, 36, 38).

Rows 1–6 G st.

Rows 7–36 (42, 45, 48) Change to larger needles. Working in St st, inc 1 st at each end of every 3rd row 10 (12, 13, 14) times — 52 (58, 62, 66) sts.

Work even until sleeve measures 6 (6.5, 7.5, 8.5)in/15 (16.5, 19, 21.5)cm, ending with WS row.

Shape Cap

BO 6 (7, 8, 8) sts at beg of next 6 rows.

BO rem 16 (16, 14, 18) sts.

NECKBAND

Sew shoulder seams.

Row 1 With RS facing, using smaller needles and Grass, K12 (13, 14, 15) sts from left back neck st holder, pick up and K14 (14, 16, 16) sts along left side of neck, K8 (10, 10, 12) sts from front holder, pick up and K14 (14, 16, 16) sts along right side of neck, K12 (13, 14, 15) sts from right back neck holder — 60 (64, 70, 74) sts.

Row 2 G st.

Row 3 Buttonhole row (RS) K to last 3 sts, yo, K2tog, K1.

Rows 4–5 G st. BO knitwise.

FINISHING

Place markers 4.75 (5.25, 5.5, 5.75)in/12 (13, 14, 15)cm from shoulder seams on both sides of front and back. Sew sleeves bet markers. Sew side and sleeve seams. Sew CO edge of left back border behind right back border to form placket. Sew on button to correspond with buttonhole. Sew two snaps evenly spaced bet button and bottom of placket.

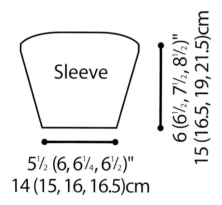

Sleeve

6 (6½, 7½, 8½)"
15 (16.5, 19, 21.5)cm

5½ (6, 6¼, 6½)"
14 (15, 16, 16.5)cm

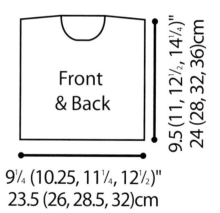

Front & Back

9.5 (11, 12½, 14¼)"
24 (28, 32, 36)cm

9¼ (10.25, 11¼, 12½)"
23.5 (26, 28.5, 32)cm

Swing Cardigan

Measurements

Size	0–6 months	6–12 months	12–18 months	
To Fit Chest	18 46	20 51	22 56	in cm
Actual Size	20 51	22 56	24 61	in cm
Full Length (approximately)	8.25 21	9.75 25	11 28	in cm
Sleeve Length (adjustable)	0.5 1	0.5 1	0.75 2	in cm
Sirdar Snuggly DK (Lilac 219)	2	3	3	1.75oz/50g; 179yds/164m

Materials

* 1 Pair US 3 (3.25mm) knitting needles
* 1 Pair US 6 (4mm) knitting needles OR SIZE TO OBTAIN GAUGE
* Stitch holders
* Stitch markers
* 1 Button
* Sewing needle and thread

Gauge

23 sts and 33 rows = 4in/10cm in patt st with larger needles. TAKE TIME TO CHECK GAUGE.

SWING CARDIGAN

BACK

Border

With smaller needles, CO 59 (65, 71).

Rows 1–4 G st.

BODY

Row 5 (RS) Change to larger needles, Knit.

Row 6 P1 (0, 3), K1, [P3, K1] to last 1 (0, 3) sts, P1 (0, 3).

Row 7 and foll RS rows Knit.

Row 8 P3 (2, 1), K1, [P3, K1] to last 3 (2, 1) sts, P3 (2, 1).

Rep last 4 Rows for patt.

Shaping Maintaining st patt as established,

Row 9 Dec 1 st at each end of row — 57 (63, 69) sts.

Rows 10–21 (21, 17) Dec 1 st at each end of every 4th (6th, 8th) row 3 (2, 1) time — 51 (59, 67) sts.

Rows — (22–29, 18–37) Dec 1 st at each end of every 0 (8th, 10th) row 0 (1, 2) times — 51(57, 63) sts.

Work even until back measures 3.5 (4.75, 6)in/9 (12, 15)cm, ending with WS row.

Shape Raglans Maintaining st patt as established,

Rows 1–2 BO 4 sts at beg of row — 43 (49, 55) sts.

Row 3 Dec 1 st at each end of next row — 41 (47, 53) sts.

Rows 4–10 (10, 6) Dec 1 st at each end of every 4th (4th, 0) row 1 (1, 0) times — 39 (45, 53) sts.

Rows 11–14 (11–16, 7–18) Dec 1 st at each end of each RS row 2 (3, 6) times — 35 (39, 41) sts.

Place rem 35 (39, 41) sts on holder.

LEFT FRONT

Border

With smaller needles, CO 36 (39, 44).

Rows 1–3 G st.

Row 4 (WS) K11 (11, 13) sts, place these 11 (11, 13) sts on holder for left front band, K to end — 25 (28, 31) sts.

BODY

Row 5 (RS) Change to larger needles, Knit.

Row 6 [P3, K1] to last 1 (0, 3) sts, P1 (0, 3).

Row 7 Knit.

Row 8 P1, [K1, P3] to last 0 (3, 2) sts, K0 (1, 1), P0 (2, 1).

Rep last 4 Rows for patt.

Shaping Maintaining st patt as established,

Row 9 Dec 1 st at beg (side edge) of row — 24 (27, 30) sts.

Rows 10–21 (21, 17) Dec 1 st at beg of every 4th (6th, 8th) row 3 (2, 1) time — 21 (25, 29) sts.

Rows — (22–29, 18–37) Dec 1 st at beg of every 0 (8th, 10th) row 0 (1, 2) times — 21 (24, 27) sts.

Work even until piece measures 3.5 (4.75, 6) in/9 (12, 15)cm, ending with WS row.

Shape Raglan Maintaining st patt as established,

Row 1 (RS) BO 4 sts at beg of row — 17 (20, 23) sts.

Row 2 Work even.

Row 3 Dec 1 st at raglan edge — 16 (19, 22) sts.

Rows 4–11 (11, 6) Dec 1 st at raglan edge every 4th (4th, 0) row 2 (2, 0) times — 14 (17, 22) sts.

Row — (12–13, 7–15) Dec 1 st at raglan edge on every RS row 0(1, 5) times — 14 (16, 17) sts. PM at neck edge.

Shape Neck Maintaining st patt as established,

Row 12 (14, 16) BO 10 (12, 13) sts, work across — 4 sts.

Row 13 (15, 17) (RS) K2tog 2 times — 2 sts.

Row 14 (16, 18) P2tog, fasten off.

LEFT FRONT BORDER

With RS facing, using smaller needles, CO 1 st, K11 (11, 13) sts from holder for left front band — 12 (12, 14) sts.

Work in G st until left front band reaches marker when slightly stretched, ending with WS row.

Place 12 (12, 14) sts on holder.

RIGHT FRONT

Border

With smaller needles, CO 36 (39, 44).

Rows 1–3 G st.

Row 4 (WS) K to last 11 (11, 13) sts, place 11 (11, 13) sts on holder for right front band — 25 (28, 31) sts.

BODY

Row 5 (RS) Change to larger needles, Knit.

Row 6 P1 (0, 3), [K1, P3] acrosss.

Row 7 Knit.

Row 8 P3 (2, 1), K1, [P3, K1] to last st, P1.

Rep last 4 Rows for patt.

Shaping Maintaining st patt as established,

Row 9 Dec 1 st at end (side edge) of row — 24 (27, 30) sts.

Rows 10–21 (21, 17) Dec 1 st at end every 4th (6th, 8th) row 3 (2, 1) times — 21 (25, 29) sts.

Rows — (22–29, 18–37) Dec 1 st at side edge of every 0 (8th, 10th) row 0 (1, 2) times — 21 (24, 27) sts.

Work even until piece measures 3.5 (4.75, 6) in/9 (12, 15)cm, ending with RS row.

Shape Raglans Maintaining st patt as established,

Row 1 BO 4 sts, work across — 17 (20, 23) sts.

Row 2 Dec 1 st at raglan edge — 16 (19, 22) sts.

Rows 3–9 (9, 5) Dec 1 st at raglan edge on every 4th (4th, 0) row (1, 1, 0) times — 15 (18, 22) sts.

Rows — (10–11, 6–13) Dec 1 st at raglan edge on every RS row 0 (1, 4) times — 15 (17, 18) sts. PM at neck edge.

Shape Neck Maintaining st patt as established,

Row 10 (12, 14) BO 10 (12, 13) sts, work to last 2 sts, K2tog — 4 sts.

Row 11 (13, 15) (WS) Work even.

Row 12 (14, 16) (RS) K2tog 2 times — sts.

Row 13 (15, 17) P2tog, fasten off.

RIGHT FRONT BORDER

With WS facing, using smaller needles, CO 1 st, K11 (11, 13) sts from holder for right front band — 12 (12, 14) sts.

Work in G st until right front band reaches marker when slightly stretched, ending with WS row. Do not cut yarn. Place 12 (12, 14) sts on holder.

SLEEVES (Make 2)

Cuff

With smaller needles, CO 41 (45, 49) sts.

Rows 1–4 G st.

Arm

Row 5 (RS) Change to larger needles, Knit.

Row 6 P2 (2, 0), K1, [P3, K1] to last 2 (2, 0) sts, P2 (2, 0).

Row 7 Knit.

Row 8 P0 (0, 2), K1, [P3, K1] to last 0 (0, 2) sts, P0 (0, 2).

Rep last 4 rows for patt.

Rows — (9–10, 9–12) Work even.

Shape Raglan Maintaining st patt as established,

Rows 9–10 (11–12, 13–14) BO 4 sts at beg of next 2 rows — 33 (37, 41) sts.

Row 11 (13, 15) Dec 1 st at each end of row — 31 (35, 39) sts.

Rows 12–18 (14–20, 16–22) Dec 1 st at each end of 4th row — 29 (33, 37) sts.

Rows 19–22 (21–26, 23–30) Dec 1 st at each end of every RS row 2 (3, 4) times — 25 (27, 29) sts.

Place rem 25 (27, 29) sts on holder.

YOKE

Sew raglan seams.

Row 1 With RS facing, using smaller needles, from holder for right front border K10 (10, 12), K2tog, pick up and K11 (13, 14) sts evenly along right side of neck, K25 (27, 29) sts from holder at top of right sleeve decreasing every 6th (6th, 7th) st 4 times, K35 (39, 41) sts from holder at back decreasing every 7th (7th, 8th) st 5 times, K25 (27, 29) sts from holder at top of left sleeve decreasing every 6th (6th, 7th) st 4 times, pick up and K11 (13, 14) sts along left side of neck, from holder for left front border K2tog, K10 (10, 12) — 116 (128, 140) sts.

Rows 2–6, 8–12, 15–18, 20–25 G st.

Row 7 (WS) K15 (12, 18), K2tog, [K4, K2tog] 14 (17, 17) times, K15 (12, 18) — 101 (110, 122) sts.

Row 13 Buttonhole row (RS) K4, BO 3 sts, K6 (4, 10), K2tog, [K3, K2tog] 14 (17, 17) times, K16 (12, 18) — 86 (92, 104)/sts.

Row 14 Knit to last 4 sts, CO 3 sts, K4.

Row 19 K14 (11, 17), K2tog, [K2, K2tog] 14 (17, 17) times, K14 (11, 17) — 71 (74, 86) sts.

Row 26 BO knitwise.

FINISHING

Sew side and sleeve seams. Sew borders to fronts through CO sts. Sew button to correspond with buttonhole.

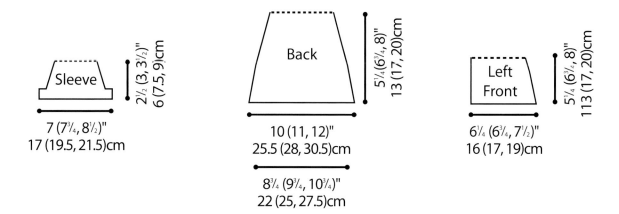

Sleeve
2½ (3, 3½)"
6 (7.5, 9)cm
7 (7¾, 8½)"
17 (19.5, 21.5)cm

Back
5¼ (6¾, 8)"
13 (17, 20)cm
10 (11, 12)"
25.5 (28, 30.5)cm
8¾ (9¾, 10¾)"
22 (25, 27.5)cm

Left Front
5¼ (6¾, 8)"
113 (17, 20)cm
6¼ (6¾, 7½)"
16 (17, 19)cm

Nautical Sweater

Measurements   Skill Level ★ ★

Size	0–3 months	3–6 months	6–12 months	12–18 months	
To Fit Chest	16 / 41	18 / 46	20 / 51	22 / 56	in / cm
Actual Size	18.5 / 47	20 / 51	22.5 / 57	25 / 63.5	in / cm
Full Length (approximately)	10.5 / 26.5	11.5 / 29	12.5 / 32	14.5 / 37	in / cm
Sleeve Length (adjustable)	6 / 15	7 / 18	7.5 / 19	8.5 / 21.5	in / cm
Debbie Bliss Mia (Marine 003)	2	2	2	3	1.75oz/50g; 109yds/100m
Debbie Bliss Mia (White 001)	2	2	2	3	1.75oz/50g; 109yds/100m
Debbie Bliss Mia (Ruby 009)	1	1	1	1	1.75oz/50g; 109yds/100m

Materials

* 1 Pair US 3 (3.25mm) knittingneedles
* 1 Pair US 6 (4mm) knitting needles OR SIZE TO OBTAIN GAUGE
* Stitch holders
* Stitch markers

Gauge

21 sts and 29 rows = 4in/10cm in St st with larger needles. TAKE TIME TO CHECK GAUGE.

SWEATER

STRIPE PATTERN Worked in St st throughout.

4 rows Marine, 4 rows White.

BACK

With smaller needles and Ruby, CO 49 (55, 61, 67).

Rows 1–2 G st.

Rows 3–66 (72, 78, 92) Change to larger needles, work stripe patt.

Shape Right Side of Neck Maintaining stripe patt,

Row 67 (73, 79, 93) K17 (19, 22, 23), place 32 (36, 39, 44) sts on holder.

Row 68 (74, 80, 94) BO 2 (2, 2, 4) sts at neck edge, P across — 15 (17, 20, 19) sts. PM at end of row to mark shoulder.

Shape Shoulder Maintaining stripe patt,

Rows 69–76 (75–82, 81–88, 95–102) Dec 1 st at neck edge of RS rows 4 times — 11 (13, 16, 15) sts.

Row 77 (83, 89, 103) BO 5 (3, 4, 4) sts at beg of row — 6 (10, 12, 11) sts.

Row 78 (84, 90, 104) and foll WS row: Purl.

Row 79 (85, 91, 105) BO 6 (4, 5, 5) sts at beg of row — 0 (6, 7, 6) sts.

Row — (87, 93, 107) BO 0 (6, 7, 6) sts.

Shape Left Side of Neck Maintaining stripe patt,

Row 67 (73, 79, 93) Move sts from holder, place center 15 (17, 17, 21) sts back on holder. Join yarn, BO 2 (2, 2, 4) sts at neck edge, K across — 15 (17, 20, 19) sts.

Row 68 (74, 80, 94) Purl. PM at beg of row to mark shoulder.

Shape Shoulder Maintaining stripe patt,

Rows 69–77 (75–83, 81–89, 95–103) Dec 1 st at neck edge of RS rows 4 times — 11 (13, 16, 15) sts.

Row 78 (84, 90, 104) BO 5 (3, 4, 4) sts at beg of row — 6 (10, 12, 11) sts.

Row 79 (85, 91, 105) and foll RS row Knit.

Row 80 (86, 92, 106) BO 6 (4, 5, 5) sts at beg of row — 0 (6, 7, 6) sts.

Row — (88, 94, 108) BO 0 (6, 7, 6) sts.

POCKET LININGS (Make 2)

With larger needles and Ruby, CO 10 (12, 14, 14).

Rows 1–12 (14, 16, 20) St st, place sts on holder and cut yarn.

FRONT

With smaller needles and Ruby, CO 49 (55, 61, 67).

Rows 1–2 G st.

Rows 2–20 (22, 24, 28) Change to larger needles, work stripe patt.

Place Pockets Maintaining stripe patt,

Row 21 (23, 25, 29) K7 (8, 8, 10) sts, place next 10 (12, 14, 14) sts on holder for pocket top, K10 (12, 14, 14) sts of 1st pocket lining from st holder, K15 (15, 17, 19) sts, place 10 (12, 14, 14) sts on holder for pocket top, K10 (12, 14, 14) sts of 2nd pocket lining from st holder, K7 (8, 8, 10) sts.

Rows 22–36 (24–44, 26–43, 30–60) Work even in stripe patt in St st.

Begin Chart Maintaining stripe patt,

Row 37 (45, 45, 61) K17 (20, 23, 26), pm, beg row 1 of chart over next 15 sts, pm, K17 (20, 23, 26).

Row 38 (46, 46, 62) P17 (20, 23, 26), work chart bet markers, P17 (20, 23, 26).

Rows 39–55 (47–63, 47–63, 63–79) Work chart as established.

Rows 56–64 (64–70, 64–75, 80–88) Work even in stripe patt.

Shape Left Side of Neck Maintaining stripe patt,

Row 65 (71, 75, 89) K17 (19, 20, 23) sts, place 32 (36, 41, 44) sts on holder.

Row 66 (72, 76, 90) Purl.

Rows 67–68 (73–74, 77–78, 91–94) Dec 1 st at neck edge every row 2 (2,2,4) times — 15 (17, 18, 19) sts. Pm at end of row to mark shoulder.

Shape Shoulder Maintaining stripe patt in St st,

Rows 69–76 (75–82, 79–88, 95–102) Dec 1 st at neck edge of RS rows 4 (4, 2, 4) — 11 (13, 16, 15) sts.

Row 77 (83, 89, 103) BO 5 (3, 4, 4) sts at beg of row — 6 (10, 12, 11) sts.

Row 78 (84, 90, 104) and foll WS row Purl.

Row 79 (85, 91, 105) BO 6 (4, 5, 5) sts at beg of row — 0 (6, 7, 6) sts.

Row — (87, 93, 107) BO 0 (6, 7, 6) sts.

Shape Right Side of Neck Maintaining stripe patt,

Row 65 (71, 75, 89) Move sts from holder, place center 15 (17, 21, 21) sts back on holder. Join yarn at neck edge, Knit across.

Row 66 (72, 76, 90) Purl.

Rows 67–68 (73–74, 77–78, 91–94) Dec 1 st at neck edge every row 2 (2, 2, 4) times — 15 (17, 18, 19) sts. Pm at end of last row to mark shoulder.

Shape Shoulder Maintaining stripe patt,

Rows 69–77 (75–83, 79–89, 95–103) Dec 1 st at neck edge of RS rows 77 (75–83, 79–89, 95–103) — 11 (13, 16, 15) sts.

Row 78 (84, 90, 104) BO 5 (3, 4, 4) sts at beg of row — 6 (10, 11, 11) sts.

Row 79 (85, 91, 105) and foll WS row Purl.

Row 80 (86, 94, 106) BO 6 (4, 5, 5) sts at beg of row — 0 (6, 7, 6) sts.

Row — (88, 92, 108) BO 0 (6, 7, 6) sts.

SLEEVES (Make 2)

With smaller needles and Ruby, CO 33 (35, 37, 39).

Rows 1–2 G st.

Rows 2–8 (10, 8, 6) Change to larger needles, beg stripe patt in St st.

Row 9 (11, 9, 7) Inc 1 st at each end of row — 35 (37, 39, 41) sts.

Anchor Chart

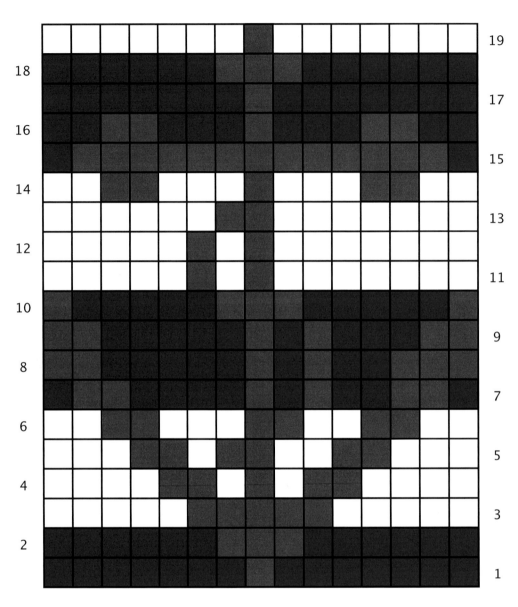

Key

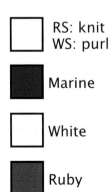

☐	RS: knit WS: purl
■	Marine
☐	White
■	Ruby

Rows 10–37 (12–35, 10–39, 8–43) Inc 1 st at each end of every 14th (8th, 6th, 6th) row 2 (3, 5, 6) times — 39 (43, 49, 53) sts.

Work even in stripe patt in St st until sleeve measures 6 (7, 7.5, 8.5)in/15 (18, 19, 21.5)cm, ending with WS row.

Shape Cap Maintaining stripe patt in St st,

BO 5 (5, 6, 5) sts at beg of next 6 (2, 2, 6) rows — 9 (33, 37, 23) sts.

BO 0 (6, 7, 6) sts at beg of next 0 (4, 4, 2) rows — 9 (9, 9, 11) sts.

BO 9 (9, 9, 11) sts.

BORDER

Back

Row 1 With RS facing, using smaller needles and Ruby, pick up and K22 (25, 27, 28) sts evenly along right side of neck, K15 (17, 17, 21) sts from holder for back of neck, pick up and K22 (25, 27, 28) sts evenly along left side of neck — 59 (67, 71, 77) sts.

Rows 2–3 G st. BO knitwise.

Front

Row 1 With RS facing, using smaller needles and Ruby, pick up and K23 (26, 28, 29) sts evenly along right side of neck, K15 (17, 21, 21) sts from holder for front of neck, pick up and K23 (26, 28, 29) sts evenly along left side of neck — 61 (69, 77, 79) sts.

Rows 2–3 G st. BO knitwise.

POCKET TOPS (Make 2)

With RS facing, using smaller needles and Ruby, K10 (12, 14, 14) sts from holder for pocket top.

BO knitwise.

FINISHING

Place back border over front border, matching shoulder markers, sew at side edge. Fold sleeves in half lengthwise and mark center of cap. Match cap marker to shoulder marker and sew sleeves in place. Sew side and sleeve seams. Slip stitch pocket linings to WS of work. Secure pocket tops at row ends.

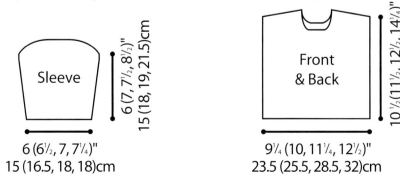

Sleeve

6 (7, 7½, 8½)"
15 (18, 19, 21.5)cm

6 (6½, 7, 7¼)"
15 (16.5, 18, 18)cm

Front
& Back

10 ½ (11½, 12½, 14¼)"
26.5 (29, 32, 37)cm

9¼ (10, 11¼, 12½)"
23.5 (25.5, 28.5, 32)cm

Zigzag Bolero

Measurements **Skill Level ★ ★**

Size	0–3 months	3–6 months	6–12 months	12–18 months	
To Fit Chest	16 41	18 46	20 51	22 56	in cm
Actual Size	19 48	21.5 55	24 61	25.5 65	in cm
Full Length (approximately)	9 23	10 26	12 30	13 33	in cm
Sleeve Length (Long Version) (adjustable)	6 15	6.5 16.5	7.5 19	8.5 21.5	in cm
Sleeve Length (Short Version) (Excluding Border)	0.75 2	1 2.5	1.25 3	1.5 3.5	in cm
Sublime Baby Cashmere Merino Silk DK (Buttermilk 345)	3	3	4	4	1.75oz/50g; 126yds/115m

Materials

* 1 Pair US 3 (3.25mm) knitting needles
* 1 Pair US 6 (4mm) knitting needles OR SIZE TO OBTAIN GAUGE
* 1 Button for flower (optional)

Gauge

22 sts and 28 rows = 4in/(10cm) in St st with larger needles. TAKE TIME TO CHECK GAUGE.

BOLERO

BACK

With larger needles CO 55 (61, 67, 71) sts.

Rows 1–28 (34, 40, 48) St st.

Shape Armholes

Rows 29–30 (35–36, 41–42, 49–50) BO 3 sts at beg of row — 49 (55, 61, 65) sts.

Row 31 (37, 43, 51) Dec 1 st at each end of row — 47 (53, 59, 63) sts.

Row 32 (38, 44, 52) Purl.

Rows 33–36 (39–44, 45–50, 53–60) Rep last 2 rows — 43 (47, 53, 55) sts.

Rows 37–60 (45–68, 51–80, 61–88) (WS) St st.

Shape Shoulders

Rows 61–62 (69–70, 81–82, 89–90) BO 6 (7, 8, 8) sts at beg of row — 31 (33, 37, 39) sts.

Rows 63–64 (71–72, 83–84, 91–92) BO 6 (7, 7, 8) sts at beg of row — 19 (19, 23, 23) sts.

BO rem 19 (19, 23, 23) sts at back of neck.

LEFT FRONT

With larger needles, CO 9.

Rows 1–5 (7, 9, 9) St st, CO 2 sts at end of RS rows — 15 (17, 19, 19) sts.

Row 6 (8, 10, 10) Purl.

Rows 7–11 (9–15, 11–19, 11–21) Inc 1 st at front edge on RS row — 18 (21, 24, 25) sts.

Row 12 (16, 20, 22) Purl.

Row 13 (17, 21, 23) Knit, inc 1 st at front edge — 19 (22, 25, 26) sts.

Rows 14–25 (18–29, 22–33, 24–39) St st, inc 1 st at front edge on every 4th row — 22 (25, 28, 30) sts.

Rows 26–28 (30–34, 34–40, 40–48) St st.

Shape Armholes and Front Edge

Row 29 (35, 41, 49) (WS) BO 3 sts, K to last 2 sts, K2tog — 18 (21, 24, 26) sts.

Row 30 (36, 42, 50) Purl.

Rows 31–35 (37–43, 43–49, 51–59) Dec 1 st at armhole on RS rows.

AT THE SAME TIME, dec 1 st at front edge on 0 (7th, 5th, 5th) row — 15 (16, 19, 20) sts.

Row 36 (44, 50, 60) Purl.

Rows 37 (45–51, 51–53, 61) Dec 1 st at front edge on next (7th, 3rd, next) row.

Rows 38–53 (52–59, 54–71, 62–79) Dec 1 st at front edge on 8th (8th, 6th, 6th) row 2 (1, 3, 3) times — 12 (14, 15, 16) sts.

Rows 54–60 (60–68, 72–78, 80–88) St st.

Shape Shoulder

Row 61 (69, 79, 89) BO 6 (7, 8, 8) sts at beg of next row — 6 (7, 7, 8) sts.

Row 62 (70, 80, 90) Purl.

Row 63 (71, 81, 91) BO rem sts.

RIGHT FRONT

With larger needles CO 9 sts.

Rows 1–6 (8, 10, 10) St st, CO 2 sts at end of WS rows — 15 (17, 19, 19) sts.

Rows 7–11 (9–15, 11–19, 11–21) Inc 1 st at front edge RS rows — 18 (21, 24, 25) sts.

Row 12 (16, 20, 22) Purl.

Row 13 (17, 21, 23) Inc 1 st at front edge, knit across — 19 (22, 25, 26) sts.

Rows 14–25 (18–29, 22–33, 24–39) Inc 1 st at front edge on every 4th row — 22 (25, 28, 30) sts.

Rows 26–29 (30–35, 34–41, 40–49) St st.

Shape Armholes and Front Edge

Row 30 (36, 42, 50) (WS) BO 3 sts, P to last 2 sts, P2tog — 18 (21, 24, 26) sts.

Rows 31–35 (37–43, 43–49, 51–59) Dec 1 st at armhole on RS rows.

AT THE SAME TIME Dec 1 st at front edge on 0 (7th, 5th, 5th) row — 15 (16, 19, 20) sts.

Row 36 (44, 50, 60) Purl.

Rows 37 (45–51, 51–53, 61) Dec 1 st at front edge on next (7th, 3rd, next) row — 14 (15, 18, 19) sts.

Rows 38–53 (52–59, 54–71, 62–79) Dec 1 st at front edge on 8th (8th, 6th, 6th) row 2 (1, 3, 3) times — 12 (14, 15, 16) sts.

Rows 54–61 (60–69, 72–79, 80–89) St st.

Shape Shoulder

Row 62 (70, 80, 90) (WS) BO 6 (7, 8, 8) sts at beg of row, purl across — 6 (7, 7, 8) sts.

Row 63 (71, 81, 91) Purl.

Row 64 (72, 82, 92) BO rem sts.

LONG SLEEVES (Make 2)

With larger needles, CO 31 (33, 35, 35) sts.

Rows 1–3 St st, inc 1 st at each end of 3rd row — 33 (35, 37, 37) sts.

Rows 4–31 St st, inc 1 st at each end of 4th row 7 times — 47 (49, 51, 51) sts.

Rows -- (32–37, 32–43, 32–55) St st, inc 1 st at each end of every 0 (6th, 6th, 6th) row 0 (1, 2, 4) times — 47 (51, 55, 59) sts.

Rows 32–38 (38–44, 44–52, 56–64) St st.

Shape Cap

** **Rows 39–40 (45–46, 53–54, 65–66) (RS)** BO 3 sts at beg of row, — 41 (45, 49, 53) sts.

Rows 41–45 (47–53, 55–61, 67–75) St st, dec 1 st at each end of next 3 (4, 4, 5) WS rows — 35 (37, 41, 43) sts.

Row 46 (54, 62, 76) Purl 1 row.

Rows 47–51 (55–58, 63–66, 77–80) BO 5 sts at beg of each row — 15 (17, 21, 23) sts. BO rem sts. **

SHORT SLEEVES (Make 2)

With larger needles, CO 47 (51, 55, 59) sts.

Rows 1–4 (6, 8, 10) St st.

Shape Cap

Work same as cap of long sleeve ** to **.

FINISHING

Sew shoulder, armhole, underarm and side seams.

SLEEVE BORDERS (Make 2) (For either sleeve length)

With smaller needles, CO 4.

Row 1 (RS) K2, yo, K2 — 5 sts.

Row 2, 4, 6 Knit.

Row 3 K3, yo, K2 — 6 sts.

Row 5 K2, yo, K2tog, yo, K2 — 7 sts.

Row 7 K3, yo, K2tog, yo, K2 — 8 sts.

Row 8 BO next 4 sts, K4.

Rep last 8 rows until straight edge fits around CO edge of sleeve, ending with Row 8, BO. Sew CO and BO edges of border tog and sew to edge of sleeve.

BODY BORDER

Work as given for sleeve border until straight edge fits around back, fronts, and neck ending with row 8. Sew to edge of sweater, stitching CO and BO edges of border tog.

FLOWER (Optional)

With smaller needles, CO 5.

Row 1 (RS) Kfb into every st.

Row 2 Purl.

Rows 3–8 Rep last 2 rows — 80 sts.

Picot BO BO 4, [slip 1 st from RH needle back to LH needle, CO 2, BO 4] to end, Fasten off.

Gather CO edge, pull up tightly and fasten off.

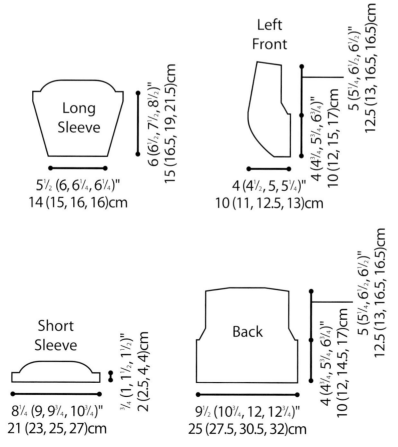

Long
Sleeve

6 (6½, 7½, 8½)"
15 (16.5, 19, 21.5)cm

5½ (6, 6¼, 6¼)"
14 (15, 16, 16)cm

Left
Front

5 (5¼, 6½, 6½)"
12.5 (13, 16.5, 16.5)cm

4 (4¾, 5¾, 6¾)"
10 (12, 15, 17)cm

4 (4½, 5, 5¼)"
10 (11, 12.5, 13)cm

Short
Sleeve

¾ (1, 1½, 1½)"
2 (2.5, 4, 4)cm

8¼ (9, 9¾, 10¾)"
21 (23, 25, 27)cm

Back

5 (5¼, 6½, 6½)"
12.5 (13, 16.5, 16.5)cm

4 (4¾, 5¾, 6¾)"
10 (12, 14.5, 17)cm

9½ (10¾, 12, 12¾)"
25 (27.5, 30.5, 32)cm

Daisy Sweater

Measurements

Size	0–6 months	6–12 months	12–18 months	
To Fit Chest	18 / 46	20 / 51	22 / 56	in / cm
Actual Size	20 / 51	22 / 56	24 / 61	in / cm
Full Length (approximately)	11 / 28	13 / 33	14 / 35	in / cm
Sleeve Length (adjustable)	6.5 / 16.5	7.5 / 19	8.5 / 21.5	in / cm
Hayfield Baby Double Knitting (Lovely in Lilac 453)	1	2	2	3.4oz/50g; 383yds/350m

Materials

* 1 Pair US 3 (3.25mm) knitting needles
* 1 Pair US 6 (4mm) knitting needles OR SIZE TO OBTAIN GAUGE
* Stitch markers
* Stitch holders

Gauge

22 sts and 28 rows = 4in/10cm in Rev St st with larger needles. TAKE TIME TO CHECK GAUGE.

SPECIAL ABBREVIATIONS

S2kpo Slip next 2 sts from LH needle to RH needle as if to K2tog, without knitting them, K next st, pass the 2 slipped sts over the K st — 2 sts decreased.

MB (Make Bobble) Knit into front, back, and front of next st, turn. P3, turn, K3, turn. P1, P2tog, turn. K2tog.

1/1 Rib (over an odd number of sts) **Row 1** K1, [P1, K1] across. **Row 2** P1, [K1, P1] across. Rep Rows 1–2.

BACK

Ruffle

With smaller needles, CO 157 (181, 193).

Row 1 (RS) Purl.

Rows 2, 4 K1, [K1, P9, K2] across.

Row 3 P1, [P1, K9, P2] across.

Row 5 P1, [P1, skpo, K5, K2tog, P2] across — 131 (151, 161) sts.

Row 6 K1, [K1, P7, K2] across.

Row 7 P1, [P1, skpo, K3, K2tog, P2] across — 105 (121, 129) sts.

Row 8 K1, [K1, P5, K2] across.

Row 9 P1, [P1, skpo, K1, K2tog, P2] across — 79 (91, 97) sts.

Row 10 K1, [K1, P3, K2] across.

Row 11 P1, [P1, s2kpo, P2] across — 53 (61, 65) sts.

Rows 12–13 Knit.

Row 14 Knit, inc 1 (0, 1) st at each end of row — 55 (61, 67) sts.

Body

Change to larger needles and set up for chart as foll:

Row 15 (RS) P2 (4, 6), pm, beg Flower Chart, pm, [P3 (4, 5), pm, beg Flower Chart, pm] 2 times, P2 (4, 6).

Row 2 K2 (4, 6), work Row 2 of Flower Chart bet markers [K3 (4, 5), Row 2 of Flower Chart bet markers] 2 times, K2 (4, 6).

Rows 3–30 Cont as established working Flower Chart.

Work even in Rev St st until body measures 6.5 (7.5, 8.5)in/16.5 (19, 21.5)cm, ending with WS row.

Shape Armholes

BO 3 sts at beg of next 2 rows — 49 (55, 61) sts.

Dec 1 st at each end of next 3 (3, 5) rows — 43 (49, 51) sts.

Dec 1 st on each end of every foll alt row 2 (3, 2) times — 39 (43, 47) sts. **

Work even until armhole measures 4.25 (4.75, 5.25)in/11 (12, 13)cm, ending with WS row.

Shape Shoulders

BO 4 (5, 5) sts at beg of next 2 rows — 31 (33, 37) sts.

BO 4 (4, 5) sts at beg of next 2 rows — 23 (25, 27) sts.

Place rem 23 (25, 27) sts on a st holder.

FRONT

Work as given for back to **.

Work even until armhole measures 2 (2.25, 2.25)in/5 (6, 6)cm or 18 (18, 20) rows less than back to start of shoulder shaping, ending with WS row.

Shape Neck – Left Front

Next Row (RS) P16 (17, 19), sl 7 (9, 9) sts on a holder, leave rem 16 (17, 19) unworked, turn.

***Dec 1 st at neck edge of next 4 rows — 12 (13, 15) sts.

Dec 1 st at neck edge of every foll alt row 3 (3, 4) times — 9 (10, 11) sts.

Dec 1 st at neck edge of 4th row — 8 (9, 10) sts.

Work even 3 rows.

Shape Shoulder

BO 4 (4, 5) sts at beg of next row.

Work 1 row.

BO rem 4 (5, 5) sts, cut yarn. ***

Shape Neck and Shoulder – Right Front

With RS facing, join yarn to work rem 16 (17, 19) unworked sts, purl across.

Rep from *** to ***, working 1 extra row before shoulder shaping.

SLEEVES (Make 2)

With smaller needles, CO 35 (37, 37).

Rows 1–6 (6, 8) 1/1 Rib.

Change to larger needles.

Rows 7–12 (7–12, 9–14) Work even in Rev St st.

Row 13 (13, 15) Inc 1 st at each end row — 37 (39, 39) sts.

Inc 1 st at each end of every 12th (12th, 14th) row 2 (2, 4) times — 41 (43, 47) sts.

Work even until sleeve measures 6.5 (7.5, 8.5)in/16.5, 19, 21.5)cm, ending with WS row.

Shape Cap

BO 3 sts at beg of next 2 rows — 35 (37, 41) sts.

Dec 1 st at each end of next row — 33 (35, 39) sts.

Work even 1 row.

Rep last 2 rows 10 (11, 11) times — 13 (13, 17) sts.

Dec 1 st at each end of next 3 (3, 5) rows — 7 sts.

BO rem 7 sts.

Flower Chart

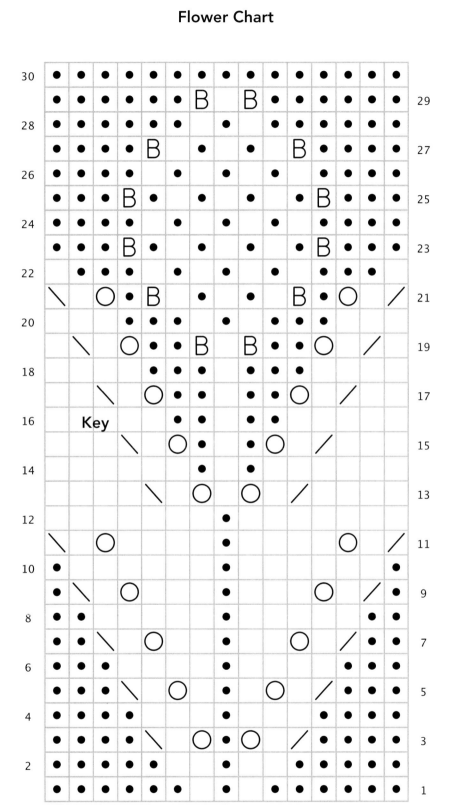

Key

☐	RS: knit WS: purl
●	RS: purl WS: knit
◯	yo
╱	K2tog
╲	skpo
B	MB

NECKBAND

Sew right shoulder seam.

With smaller needles and RS facing, pick up and K18 (18, 20) sts evenly along left side of neck, knit across sts from front st holder, pick up and K18 (18, 20) sts evenly along right side of neck, knit across sts from back st holder, dec 1 st at center back neck — 65 (69, 75) sts.

Rows 1–5 (5, 7) 1/1 Rib.

BO in rib.

FINISHING

Sew left shoulder and neckband seam. Fold sleeves in half lengthwise and mark center of cap. Match marker to shoulder seam and sew sleeves in place. Sew side and sleeve seams.

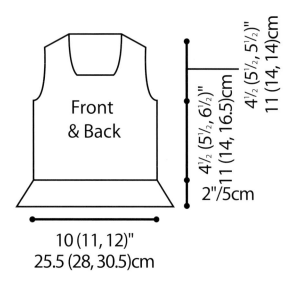

Front & Back

4½ (5½, 6½)"
11 (14, 16.5)cm

4½ (5½, 5½)"
11 (14, 14)cm

2"/5cm

10 (11, 12)"
25.5 (28, 30.5)cm

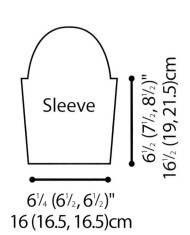

Sleeve

6½ (7½, 8½)"
16½ (19, 21.5)cm

6¼ (6½, 6½)"
16 (16.5, 16.5)cm

Striped Cardigan

Measurements **Skill Level ★ ★**

Size	0–3 months	3–6 months	6–12 months	12–18 months	
To Fit Chest	16 41	18 46	20 51	22 56	in cm
Actual Size	18 46	20 51	22 56	24 61	in cm
Full Length (approximately)	9.5 24	10.75 27	11.5 29	13.5 34	in cm
Sleeve Length (adjustable)	6 15	6.5 16.5	7.5 19	8.5 21.5	in cm
Plymouth Yarn Dreambaby DK (White 100)	1	1	2	2	1.75oz/50g; 183yds/167m
Plymouth Yarn Dreambaby DK (Green 143)	1	1	2	2	1.75oz/50g; 183yds/167m

Materials

* 1 Pair US 3 (3.25mm) knitting needles
* 1 Pair US 6 (4mm) knitting needles OR SIZE TO OBTAIN GAUGE
* 1 US 3 (3.25mm) 32in/80cm circular needle
* Stitch holders
* 4 (4, 5, 6) Buttons
* Sewing needle and thread

Gauge

22 sts and 30 rows = 4in/10cm in St st with larger needles. TAKE TIME TO CHECK GAUGE. TO CHECK GAUGE.

SPECIAL ABBREVIATIONS

1/1 Rib (over an odd number of sts) **Row 1** K1, [P1, K1] across. **Row 2** P1, [K1, P1] across. Rep Rows 1–2.

Slip next st from LHN to RHN as if to Knit, without knitting it, K next st, pass slipped st over the K st — 1 st decreased.

Rib2tog K2tog or P2tog as necessary to maintain ribbing.

STRIPED CARDIGAN

Stripe Patt

2 rows White, 2 rows Green in St st.

BACK

With smaller needles and White, CO 55 (63, 67, 75).

Row 1 (RS) 1/1 Rib.

Rows 2–8 Change to Green, 1/1 Rib.

Change to larger needles, begin stripe patt. Work even until back measures 5.5 (6.5, 6.75, 8.5)in/14 (16.5, 17, 21.5)cm, ending with WS row.

Shape Armholes – Maintaining stripe patt,

Rows 1–2 BO 2 (3, 3, 4) sts at beg of row — 51 (57, 61, 67) sts.

Row 3 (RS) K2, skpo, K to last 4 sts, K2tog, K2 — 2 sts dec.

Row 4 Purl.

Rows 5–8 (10, 10, 12) Rep last 2 rows — 45 (49, 53, 57) sts.

Rows 9–30 (11–32, 11–36, 13–38) Work even or until armhole measures 4 (4.25, 4.75, 5)in/10 (11, 12, 12.5)cm, ending with WS row.

Shape Shoulders – Maintaining stripe patt,

Rows 31–32 (33–34, 37–38, 39–40) BO 7 (7, 8, 8) sts at beg of row.

Rows 33–34 (35–36, 39–40, 41–42) BO 6 (7, 7, 8) sts at beg of row.

Place rem 19 (21, 23, 25) sts on holder.

LEFT FRONT

With smaller needles and White, CO 25 (27, 31, 33).

Row 1 (RS) 1/1 Rib.

Rows 2–8 Change to green, 1/1 Rib.

Change to larger needles, begin stripe patt. Work even until left front measures 5.5 (6.5, 6.75, 8.5)in/14 (16.5, 17, 21.5)cm, ending with WS row.

Shape Armhole – Maintaining stripe patt,

Row 1 (RS) BO 2 (3, 3, 4), knit — 23 (24, 28, 29) sts.

Row 2 Purl.

Shape Neck – Maintaining stripe patt,

Row 3 (RS) K2, skpo, K to last 4 sts, K2tog, K2 — 2 sts dec.

Row 4 Purl.

Row 5 K2, skpo, K to end — 1 st dec.

Row 6 Purl.

Rows 7–10 (10, 10, 14) Rep the last 4 rows — 17 (18, 22, 20) sts.

Rows 11-12 Rep rows 3–4 — 15 (18, 22, 20) sts.

Dec 1 st at neck edge on 4th (next, next, 4th) row — 14 (17, 21, 19) sts.

Dec 1 st at neck edge on every 6th (4th, 4th, 6th) row 1 (3, 6, 3) times — 13 (14, 15, 16) sts.

Work even until armhole measures 4 (4.25, 4.75, 5)in/10 (11, 12, 12.5)cm, ending with WS row.

Shape Shoulder – Maintaining stripe patt,

BO 7 (7, 8, 8) sts at beg of next row and 6 (7, 7, 8) sts at beg of foll row.

RIGHT FRONT

Work to match first side, reversing shaping.

SLEEVES (Make 2)

With smaller needles and White, CO 33 (35, 35, 37).

Row 1 (RS) 1/1 Rib.

Rows 2–8 Change to green, 1/1 Rib.

Change to larger needles, begin Stripe patt.

Shape Sleeve – Maintaining Stripe patt,

Kfb at each end of 3rd row — 35 (37, 37, 39) sts.

Kfb at each end of every 4th row 7 (8, 10, 11) times — 49 (53, 57, 61) sts.

Work even until sleeve measures 6 (6.5, 7.5, 8.5)in/15 (16.5, 19, 21.5)cm, ending with RS row.

Shape Cap – Maintaining stripe patt,

BO 2 (3, 3, 4) sts at beg of next 2 rows — 45 (47, 51, 53) sts.

Next row (RS) K2, skpo, K to last 4 sts, K2tog, K2 — 2 sts dec.

Next row Purl.

Rep last 2 rows 2 (3, 3, 4) times — 39 (39, 43, 43) sts.

BO rem 39 (39, 43, 43) sts.

BORDER

Sew shoulder seams.

Row 1 With RS facing, circular needle and Green, pick up and K37 (43, 49, 57) sts along right front to beg of neck shaping, pick up and K27 (31, 35, 39) sts to shoulder, K 19 (21, 23, 25) sts from back neck holder, pick up and K27 (31, 35, 39) sts to start of neck shaping, pick up and K37 (43, 49, 57) sts along left front to CO edge — 147 (169, 191, 217) sts.

Rows 2–4 1/1 Rib.

For Boy's

Row 5 Buttonhole row (RS) Work ribbing to last 32 (38, 45, 50) sts, yo, Rib2tog, [work 7 (9, 8, 7) sts in ribbing, yo, rib2tog] 3 (3, 4, 5) times, work last 3 sts in ribbing.

For Girl's

Row 5 Buttonhole row (RS) Work 3 sts in ribbing, [Rib2tog, yo, work 7 (9, 8, 7) sts in ribbing] 3 (3, 4, 5) times, Rib2tog, yo, work in ribbing to end.

All Versions

Rows 6–8 1/1 Rib. BO in rib.

FINISHING

Fold sleeves in half lengthwise and mark center of cap. Match marker to shoulder seam and sew sleeves in place. Sew side and sleeve seams. Sew on buttons to correspond with buttonholes.

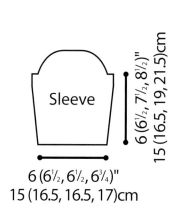

Sleeve

6 (6½, 7½, 8½)"
15 (16.5, 19, 21.5)cm

6 (6½, 6½, 6¾)"
15 (16.5, 16.5, 17)cm

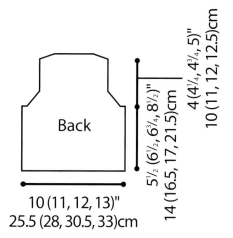

Back

4 (4¼, 4¾, 5)"
10 (11, 12, 12.5)cm

5½ (6½, 6¾, 8½)"
14 (16.5, 17, 21.5)cm

10 (11, 12, 13)"
25.5 (28, 30.5, 33)cm

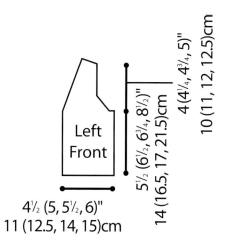

Left Front

4 (4¼, 4¾, 5)"
10 (11, 12, 12.5)cm

5½ (6½, 6¾, 8½)"
14 (16.5, 17, 21.5)cm

4½ (5, 5½, 6)"
11 (12.5, 14, 15)cm

Moss Stitch Duffle Coat

Measurements   Skill Level ★ ★

Size	0–3 months	3–6 months	6–12 months	12–18 months	
To Fit Chest	16 41	18 46	20 51	22 56	in cm
Actual Size	20 51	22.5 57	23.5 60	26 66	in cm
Full Length (approximately)	10.25 26	11.75 30	13.75 35	16 41	in cm
Sleeve Length (adjustable)	5.5 14	6 15	7.25 18	9 23	in cm
Lion Brand Baby's First (Splish Splash 106)	4	4	5	6	3.5oz/50g; 120yds/110m

Materials

* 1 Pair US 10.5 (6.5mm) knitting needles OR SIZE TO OBTAIN GAUGE
* Stitch holders
* 1 US 3 (3.25mm) 32in/80cm circular needle
* 4 (4, 6, 6) Buttons
* Sewing needle and thread

Gauge

13 sts and 23 rows – 4in (10cm) in Seed St. TAKE TIME TO CHECK GAUGE.

SPECIAL ABBREVIATIONS

Seed st (over an odd number of sts) K1 [P1, K1] across. (Knit the purls, purl the knits).

M3K — (Knit into front, purl into back, knit into front) all in next st (2 sts increased).

M3P — (Purl into front, knit into back, purl into front) all into next st (2 sts increased).

BOY'S VERSION

BACK

CO 33 (37, 39, 43) sts.

Rows 1–56 (64, 76, 90) Seed st.

Shape Shoulders Maintain Seed st.

Rows 57–58 (65–66, 77–78, 91–92) BO 5 (6, 6, 4) sts at beg of row — 23 (25, 27, 35) sts.

Rows 59–60 (66–67, 79–80, 93–96) BO 6 (6, 6, 5) sts at beg of row — 11 (13, 15, 15) sts.

Place 11 (13, 15, 15) sts on holder.

POCKET LININGS (make 2)

CO 9 (9, 11, 11) sts.

Rows 1–16 (16, 18, 20) Seed st.

Place 9 (9, 11, 11) sts on holder.

RIGHT FRONT

CO 21 (23, 25, 27) sts.

Rows 1–21 (23, 25, 29) Seed st.

Place Pocket Maintaining st patt,

Row 22 (24, 26, 30) Work 3 sts, BO next 9 (9, 11, 11) sts knitwise, work in patt to end.

Row 23 (25, 27, 31) (RS) Work 9 (11, 11, 13) sts, work sts of pocket lining from st holder as foll: P1, [K1, P1] 4 (4, 5, 5) times, K1, P1, K1.

Rows 24–50 (26–58, 28–70, 32–82) Work even in Seed st.

Shape Neck Maintaining st patt,

Row 51 (59, 71, 83) BO 7 (8, 10, 10) sts, work across — 14 (15, 15, 17) sts.

Row 52 (60, 72, 84) Work even.

Rows 53–55 (61–63, 73–75, 85–87) Dec 1 st at neck edge — 11 (12, 12, 14) sts.

Rows 56–57 (64–65, 76–77, 88–91) Work even.

Shape Shoulder Maintaining st patt,

Row 58 (66, 78, 92) BO 5 (6, 6, 4) sts at beg of row — 6 (6, 6, 10) sts.

Row 60 (68, 80, 94–96) BO 6 (6, 6, 5) sts at beg of next 1 (1, 1, 2) WS rows.

LEFT FRONT

CO 21 (23, 25, 27) sts.

Rows 1–21 (23, 25, 29) (RS) Seed st.

Place Pocket Maintaining st patt,

Row 22 (24, 26, 30) Work 9 (11, 11, 13) sts, BO next 9 (9, 11, 11) sts knitwise, K1, P1, K1.

Row 23 (25, 27, 31) (RS) Work 3 sts, work sts of pocket lining from st holder as foll: P1, [K1, P1] 4 (4, 5, 5) times, work across.

Rows 24–30 (26–34, 28–38, 32–42) Work even in Seed st.

Row 31 (35, 39, 43) Buttonhole row (RS) Work 11 (11, 13, 13) sts, P2tog, yo, work 3 (5, 5, 7) sts, K2tog, yo, K1, P1, K1.

Rows 32–46 (36–54, 40–52, 44–60) Work even in Seed st.

Row 47 (55, 53, 61) (RS) Rep Buttonhole row.

Rows 48–51 (56–59, 54–66, 62–78) Work even in Seed st.

Row -- (--, 67, 79) Work 0 (0, 13, 13) sts, P2tog, yo, work 0 (0, 5, 7), K2tog, yo, K1, P1, K1.

Rows -- (--, 68–71, 80–83) Work even in Seed st.

Shape Neck Maintaining st patt,

Row 52 (60, 72, 84) BO 7 (8, 10, 10) sts, work across — 14 (15, 15, 17) sts.

Rows 53–55 (61–63, 73–75, 85–87) Dec 1 st at neck edge — 11 (12, 12, 14) sts.

Row 56 (64, 76, 88–90) Work even in Seed st.

Shape Shoulder Maintaining st patt,

Row 57 (65, 77, 91) BO 5 (6, 6, 4) sts at beg of row — 6 (6, 6, 10) sts.

Row 58 (66, 68, 92) Work even in Seed st.

Row 59 (67, 69, 93) BO 6 (6, 6, 5) sts at beg of row — 0 (0, 0, 5) sts.

Rows -- (--, --, 94–95) Rep last 2 rows.

SLEEVES (Make 2)

CO 19 (21, 23, 25) sts.

Rows 1–10 (10, 8, 10) Seed st.

Row 11 (11, 9, 11) Maintaining st patt, inc 1 st at each end of row — 21 (23, 25, 27) sts.

Rows 12–27 (12–31, 10–37, 12–47) Maintaining st patt, inc 1 st at each end of every 16th (10th, 14th, 12th) row 1 (2, 2, 3) times — 23 (27, 29, 33) sts.

Rows 28–32 (32–36, 38–42, 48–52) Work even in Seed st.

Shape Cap Maintaining st patt,

Rows 33–40 (37–46, 43–52, 53–64) BO 2 sts at beg of next row — 7 (7, 9, 9) sts.

BO rem 7 (7, 9, 9) sts.

HOOD

Sew shoulder seams.

CO 13 (13, 15, 15), loosely.

Row 1 P1, [K1, P1] 6 (6, 7, 7) times, with RS facing, work sts from holder at back of neck as folls: (K1, P1) 1 (2, 2, 2) times, K1 (0, 0, 0), M3P (M3K, M3K, M3K), K1 (0, 0, 0), (P1, K1) 1 (1, 2, 2) times, P0 (1, 1, 1), M3P (M3K, M3K, M3K), K1 (0, 0, 0), (P1, K1) 1 (2, 2, 2) times, CO 13 (13, 15, 15) sts loosely — 41 (43, 49, 49) sts.

Rows 2–32 (34, 36, 40) Work even in Seed st.

Shape Crown Maintaining st patt,

Rows 33-34 (35–36, 37–38, 41–42) BO 14 (14, 16, 16) sts at beg of row — 13 (15, 17, 17) sts.

Rows 35–52 (37–56, 39–62, 43–66) Work even in Seed st.

BO in Seed st.

HOOD BORDER

Sew seams on hood.

Row 1 With RS facing, pick up and K22 (24, 26, 27) sts evenly along right side of hood, pick up and K12 (14, 15, 16) sts at crown, pick up and K 22 (24, 26, 27) sts evenly along left side of hood — 56 (62, 67, 70) sts.

Rows 2–3 G st.

BO knitwise.

FINISHING

PM on each side of front and back 4 (4.25, 4.75, 5.25)in/10 (11, 12, 13) cm from shoulder seams. Fold sleeves in half lengthwise and mark center of cap. Match sleeve cap marker to shoulder seam. Sew sleeves in place bet body markers. Sew side and sleeve seams. Sew hood border evenly along neck edge. Sew pocket linings to WS. Sew buttons to correspond to buttonholes.

GIRL'S VERSION Work same as given for boy's version except:

RIGHT FRONT

Work Rows 1–30 (34, 38, 42) of Boy's Right front.

Row 31 (35, 39, 43) Buttonhole row (RS) K1, P1, K1, yo, K2tog, work 3 (5, 5, 7), yo, P2tog, work 11 (11, 13, 13).

Rows 32–50 (36–58, 40–70, 44–82) Continue as for Boy's Left Front, using Girl's Buttonhole Row.

Rows 51–60 (59–68, 71–80, 83–96 Continue as for Boys Right Front.

Continue as for Boy's Left Front using Girl's Buttonhole row.

LEFT FRONT

Work same as Boy's Left Front, omitting buttonholes.

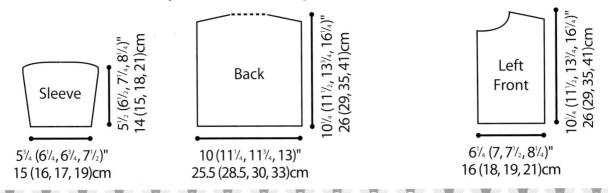

Sleeve

5½ (6½, 7¼, 8¼)"
14 (15, 18, 21)cm

5¾ (6¼, 6¾, 7½)"
15 (16, 17, 19)cm

Back

10¼ (11½, 13¾, 16¼)"
26 (29, 35, 41)cm

10 (11¼, 11¾, 13)"
25.5 (28.5, 30, 33)cm

Left Front

10¼ (11½, 13¾, 16¼)"
26 (29, 35, 41)cm

6¼ (7, 7½, 8¼)"
16 (18, 19, 21)cm

Peplum Coat

Measurements   Skill Level ★ ★

Size	0–6 months	6–12 months	12–18 months	
To Fit Chest	18 46	20 51	22 56	in cm
Actual Size	20 51	22 56	24 61	in cm
Full Length (approximately)	11 28	11.75 30	12.5 32	in cm
Sleeve Length (adjustable)	6.5 16.5	7.5 19	8.5 21.5	in cm
James C. Brett Supreme Baby 4ply (Pea Green SY7)	2	2	2	3.5oz/50g; 481yds/440m

Materials

* 1 Pair US 2 (2.75mm) knitting needles
* 1 Pair US 3 (3.25mm) knitting needles OR SIZE TO OBTAIN GAUGE
* Stitch markers
* Stitch holders
* 6 Buttons
* Sewing needle and thread

Gauge

28 sts and 36 rows = 4in/10cm in St st with larger needles. TAKE TIME TO CHECK GAUGE.

SPECIAL ABBREVIATIONS

Seed st (over an odd number of sts) K1, [P1, K1] across. (Knit the purls, purl the knits).

Patt2tog K2tog or P2tog as necessary to maintain Seed st pattern.

BACK

With smaller needles, CO 119 (131, 139) sts.

Rows 1–4 Seed st.

Change to larger needles, work even in St st until back measures 6.25 (6.75, 6.75) in/16 (17, 17)cm, ending with WS row.

Shape Bodice

Row 1 (RS) K3 (5, 7), K1, K3tog 28 (30, 31) times, K4 (6, 8) — 63 (71, 77) sts.

Rows 2–4 G st.

Work even in Seed st until back measures 7 (7.5, 8)in/18 (19, 20)cm, ending with WS row.

Shape Armholes Maintaining Seed st,

Dec 1 st at each end of next 5 (6, 7) rows — 53 (59, 63) sts.

Work even in Seed st until armhole measures 4 (4.25, 4.5)in/10 (11, 11)cm, ending with WS row.

Shape Shoulders Maintaining Seed st,

BO 7 (8, 8) sts at beg of next 2 rows — 39 (43, 47) sts.

BO 8 (9, 9) sts at beg of next 2 rows — 23 (25, 29) sts.

BO rem 23 (25, 29) sts.

LEFT FRONT

With smaller needles CO 69 (75, 81) sts.

Rows 1–3 Seed st.

Row 4 (WS) Work 19 (19, 23) sts in Seed st and sl onto holder for left front band, cont Seed st across — 50 (56, 58) sts.

Change to larger needles, work even in St st until left front measures 6.25 (6.75, 6.75)in/16 (17, 17)cm, ending with WS row.

Shape Bodice

Row 1 (RS) K5, K3tog 13 (15, 15) times, K2tog, K4 (4, 6) — 23 (25, 27) sts.

Rows 2–4 G st.

Work even in Seed st until left front measures 7 (7.5, 8)in/18 (19, 20)cm, ending with WS row.

Shape Armholes Maintaining Seed st,

Seed st across, dec 1 st at armhole edge — 22 (24, 26) sts.

Dec 1 st at armhole edge of next 4 (5, 6) rows — 18 (19, 20) sts.

Work even in Seed st until armhole measures 2.25 (2.75, 3)in/5.5 (7, 7.5)cm, ending with WS row.

Shape Neck Maintaining Seed st,

Dec 1 st at neck edge of next 3 (2, 3) rows — 15 (17, 17) sts.

Work even in Seed st until armhole measures 4 (4.25, 4.5)in/10 (11, 11)cm, ending with WS row.

Shape Shoulder Maintaining Seed st.

BO 7 (8, 8) sts at beg of next row.

Work 1 row in Seed st.

BO 8 (9, 9) sts at beg of next row.

RIGHT FRONT

With smaller needles CO 69 (75, 81) sts.

Rows 1–3 Seed st.

Row 4 (WS) Work Seed st to last 19 (19, 23), sl 19 (19, 23) sts onto holder for right front band — 50 (56, 58) sts.

Change to larger needles, work even in St st until right front measures 6.25 (6.75, 6.75)in/16 (17, 17)cm, ending with WS row.

Shape Bodice

Row 1 (RS) K4 (4, 6), K2tog, K3tog 13 (15, 15) times, K5 — 23 (25, 27) sts.

Rows 2–4 G st.

Work even in Seed st until right front measures 7 (7.5, 8)in/18 (19, 20)cm, ending with RS row.

Shape Armholes, Neck and Shoulder

Work as for Left Front, reversing shaping.

SLEEVES (Make 2)

With smaller needles, CO 37 (39, 41).

Rows 1–6 Seed st.

Change to larger needles, cont maintaining St st.

Inc 1 st at each end of 3rd (5th, 7th) row — 39 (41, 43) sts.

Inc 1 st at each end of every 6th (6th, 4th) 6 (8, 3) times — 51 (57, 49) sts.

Inc 1 st at each end of 6th row 0 (0, 6) times — 51 (57, 61) sts.

Work even in Seed st until sleeve measures 6.5 (7.5, 8.5)in/16.5 (19, 21.5)cm, ending with WS row.

Shape Cap Maintaining Seed st,

Dec 1 st at each end of next 5 (6, 7) rows — 41 (45, 47) sts.

Pm at each end of last row.

Work even 1 (0, 1) row.

BO 7 (8, 6) sts at beg of next 2 rows — 27 (29, 35) sts.

BO 8 (9, 6) sts at beg of next 2 (2, 4) rows — 11 sts.

BO rem 11 sts.

LEFT FRONT BORDER

Sew both shoulder seams.

With RS facing and using smaller needles, join yarn and work 19 (19, 23) sts from holder.

Work even in Seed st until border measures 8.5 (9.5, 10.25)in/21.5 (24, 26)cm or to match front edge to beg of neck shaping when slightly stretched, ending with WS row.

BO 6 (6, 10) sts, pm in last BO st, BO rem sts.

Sew border evenly to front. Pm for 6 buttons, with two 6.75 (7, 7)in/17 (18, 18)cm up from lower edge, 4 sts in from each edge of border, two 0.75in/2cm below BO edge and two evenly spaced between them as illustrated.

RIGHT FRONT BORDER

With WS facing and using smaller needles, join yarn and work 19 (19, 23) sts from holder. Work even in Seed st until the border measures 6.75 (7, 7)in/17 (18, 18)cm when slightly stretched, ending with WS row.

Buttonhole row (RS) Maintaining Seed st, work 4 sts, yo, patt2tog, work 7 (7, 11) sts, patt2tog, yo, work 4 sts.

Work even in Seed st, working buttonholes to correspond with markers on left front border. Cont until border measures same as left front border, ending with WS row.

BO 13 sts, pm in last BO st, BO rem sts.

COLLAR

Row 1 With RS facing and using larger needles, pick up and K27 (27, 29) sts evenly along right front neck bet marker and shoulder seam, pick up and K23 (25, 29) sts from back of neck, pick up and K27 (27, 29) sts evenly along left side of neck bet shoulder seam and marker — 77 (79, 87) sts.

Rows 2–9 (11, 13) St st.

Row 10 (12, 14) (RS) K2tog, K to last 2 sts, K2tog — 75 (77, 85) sts.

Row 11 (13, 15) Purl.

Rows 12–13 (14–15, 16–17) Rep the last 2 rows — 73 (75, 83) sts.

Rows 14–17 (16–19, 18–21) Work in St st, dec 1 st at each end of row — 65 (67, 75) sts. Cut yarn, leave sts on needle.

Row 18 (20, 22) With RS facing and using smaller needles, starting at marker, pick up and K17 (19, 21) sts evenly along right side of collar, K 65 (67, 75) sts on LH needle, pick up and K17 (19, 21) sts evenly along left side of collar to marker — 99 (105, 117) sts.

Rows 19–22 (21–24, 23–26) Seed st, ending with RS.

BO in Seed st.

FINISHING

Fold sleeves in half lengthways, matching center of fold with shoulder seam. Sew sleeves in place. Join side and sleeve seams. Sew borders in place. Sew on buttons to correspond with buttonholes.

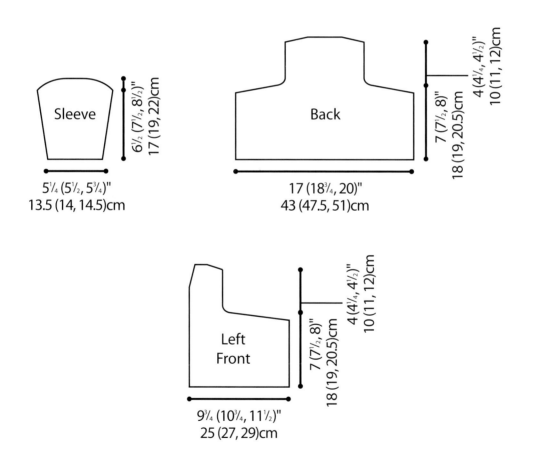

Sleeve

6½ (7½, 8½)"
17 (19, 22)cm

5¼ (5½, 5¾)"
13.5 (14, 14.5)cm

Back

4 (4¼, 4½)"
10 (11, 12)cm

7 (7½, 8)"
18 (19, 20.5)cm

17 (18¾, 20)"
43 (47.5, 51)cm

Left Front

4 (4¼, 4½)"
10 (11, 12)cm

7 (7½, 8)"
18 (19, 20.5)cm

9¾ (10¾, 11½)"
25 (27, 29)cm

Fringed Cardigan

Measurements   Skill Level ★ ★

Size	0–3 months	3–6 months	6–12 months	12–18 months	
To Fit Chest	16 / 41	18 / 46	20 / 51	22 / 56	in / cm
Actual Size	19.25 / 49	21 / 53	22.75 / 58	25.25 / 64	in / cm
Full Length (approximately)	9.5 / 24	10.5 / 26.5	11.5 / 29	13.5 / 34	in / cm
Sleeve Length (adjustable)	6 / 15	6.5 / 16.5	7.5 / 19	8.5 / 21.5	in / cm
King Cole Comfort DK (Lupin 780)	1	1	2	2	3.5oz/100g; 340yds/310m

Materials

* 1 Pair US 3 (3.75mm) knitting needles
* 1 Pair US 6 (4mm) knitting needles OR SIZE TO OBTAIN GAUGE
* 5 Buttons
* Sewing needle and thread

Gauge

23 sts and 29 rows = 4in/10cm in St st with larger needles.

SPECIAL ABBREVIATIONS

FR (Fringe) CO 5 sts on LH needle with two-needle method, BO 5 sts, leaving 1 st on RH needle.

BACK

With smaller needles, CO 53 (57, 63, 69) sts.

Rows 1–2, 4–6, 8 Knit.

Row 3 (RS) K2 (4, 3, 2), FR, [K3, FR] to last 2 (4, 3, 2) sts, K2 (4, 3, 2).

Row 7 K4 (2, 1, 4), FR, [K3, FR] to last 4 (2, 1, 4) sts, K4 (2, 1, 4).

Rows 9–12 Rep Rows 1–4.

Rows 13–38 (46, 50, 62) Change to larger needles, St st.

Shape Raglans

Rows 39–40 (47–48, 51–52, 63–64) BO 2 (3, 3, 4) sts at beg of row — 49 (51, 57, 61) sts.

Row 41 (49, 53, 65) (RS) K2, skpo, K to last 4 sts, K2tog, K2 — dec 2 sts.

Row 42 (50, 54, 66) K2, P to last 2 sts, K2.

Rows 43–70 (51–78, 55–86, 67–102) Rep the last 2 rows 14 (14, 16, 18) times — 19 (21, 23, 23) sts.

Row 71 (79, 87, 103) BO rem 19 (21, 23, 23) sts.

LEFT FRONT

With smaller needles, CO 24 (26, 29, 32).

Rows 1–2, 4–6, 8 Knit.

Row 3 (RS) K2 (4, 3, 2), FR, [K3, FR] to last st, K1.

Row 7 K4 (2, 1, 4), FR, [K3, FR] to last 3 sts, K3.

Rows 9–12 Rep Rows 1–4.

Rows 13–38 (46, 50, 62) Change to larger needles, St st.

Shape Raglan

Row 39 (47, 51, 63) (RS) BO 2 (3, 3, 4) sts, K across — 22 (23, 26, 28) sts.

Row 40 (48, 52, 64) Purl.

Row 41 (49, 53, 65) (RS) K2, skpo, K across — dec 1 st.

Row 42 (50, 54, 66) P to last 2 sts, K2.

Rows 43–56 (51–64, 55–72, 67–88) Rep the last 2 rows 7 (7, 9, 11) times — 14 (15, 16, 16) sts.

Row 57 (65, 73, 89) K2, skpo, K across — 13 (14, 15, 15) sts.

Shape Neck

Row 58 (66, 74, 90) (WS) BO 2 (3, 4, 4) sts, P to last 2 sts, K2 — 11 sts.

Row 59 (67, 75, 91) (RS) K2, skpo, K to last 2 sts, k2tog — dec 2 sts.

Row 60 (68, 76, 92) and foll WS rows P to last 2 sts, K2.

Row 61 (69, 77, 93) K2, skpo, K across — dec 1 st.

Rows 63–68 (71–76, 79–84, 95–100) Rep Rows 59–62, then Rows 59–60.

Row 69 (77, 85, 101) Knit.

Row 71 (79, 87, 103) (RS) K1, skpo — 2 sts.

Row 72 (80, 88, 104) K2tog, fasten off.

RIGHT FRONT

With smaller needles, CO 24 (26, 29, 32).

Rows 1–2, 4–6, 8 Knit.

Row 3 (RS) K1, FR, [K3, FR] to last 2 (4, 3, 2) sts, K2 (4, 3, 2).

Row 7 K3, FR, [K3, FR] to last 4 (2, 1, 4) sts, K4 (2, 1, 4).

Rows 9–12 Rep Rows 1–4.

Rows 13–39 (47, 51, 63) Change to larger needles, St st.

Shape Raglan

Row 40 (48, 52, 64) (WS) BO 2 (3, 3, 4) sts, P across — 22 (23, 26, 28) sts.

Row 41 (49, 53, 65) (RS) K to last 4 sts, K2tog, K2 — dec 1 st.

Row 42 (50, 54, 66) K2, P across.

Rows 43–56 (51–64, 55–72, 67–88) Rep the last 2 rows 7 (7, 9, 11) times — 14 (15, 16, 16) sts.

Shape Neck

Row 57 (65, 73, 89) (RS) BO 2 (3, 4, 4) sts, K to last 4 sts, K2tog, K2 — 11 sts.

Row 58 (66, 74, 90) and foll WS rows K2, P across.

Row 59 (67, 75, 91) (RS) Skpo, K to last 4 sts, K2tog, K2 — dec 2 sts.

Row 61 (69, 77, 93) K to last 4 sts, K2tog, K2 — dec 1 st.

Rows 63–68 (71–76, 79–84, 95–100) Rep Rows 59–62, then Rows 59–60.

Row 69 (77, 85, 101) Knit.

Row 70 (78, 86, 102) (WS) Skpo, K1 — 2 sts.

Row 71 (79, 87, 103) K2tog, fasten off.

SLEEVES (Make 2)

With smaller needles, CO 29 (29, 31, 31) sts.

Rows 1–2, 4–6, 8 Knit.

Row 3 (RS) K2 (2, 3, 3), FR, [K3, FR] to last 2 (2, 3, 3) sts, K2 (2, 3, 3).

Row 7 K4 (4, 1, 1), FR, [K3, FR] to last 3 (3, 1, 1) sts, K3 (3, 1, 1).

Rows 9–12 Rep Rows 1–4.

Rows 13–14 Change to larger needles, St st.

Row 15 (RS) K2, m1, K to last 2 sts, m1, K2 — inc 2 sts.

Row 16 Purl.

Rows 17–40 (44, 48, 60) Rep last 4 rows 6 (7, 8, 11) times — 43 (45, 49, 55) sts.

Work even in St st until sleeve measures 6 (6.5, 7.5, 8.5)in/15 (16.5, 19, 21.5)cm, ending with WS row.

Shape Raglans

BO 2 (3, 3, 4) sts at beg of next 2 rows — 39 (39, 43, 47) sts.

Row 1 (RS) K2, skpo, K to last 4 sts, K2tog, K2 — dec 2 sts.

Row 2 K2, P to last 2 sts, K2.

Rep the last 2 rows 14 (14, 16, 18) times — 9 sts rem.

BO rem 9 sts.

LEFT FRONT BORDER

Row 1 With RS facing, using smaller needles, pick up and K43 (51, 59, 67) sts evenly along left front edge.

Rows 2–7 G st.

BO in knitwise.

RIGHT FRONT BORDER

Row 1 With RS facing, using smaller needles, pick up and K43 (51, 59, 67) sts evenly along right front edge.

Rows 2–4 G st.

Row 5 Buttonhole row (RS) K2, [K2tog, yo, K7 (9, 11, 13)] 4 times, K2tog, yo, K3.

Rows 6–7 G st.

BO in knitwise.

COLLAR

Sew raglan seams.

Row 1 With RS facing, using smaller needles, pick up and K6 sts from top of right front border, pick up and K17 (18, 19, 19) sts evenly along right side of neck, pick up and K9 sts from top of right sleeve, 23 (25, 27, 27) sts evenly across BO sts at back of neck, 9 sts from top of left sleeve, pick up and K17 (18, 19, 19) sts evenly along left side of neck, pick up and K6 sts from top of left front border — 87 (91, 95, 95) sts.

Rows 2–3 BO 4 sts, knit — 79 (83, 87, 87) sts.

Rows 4–12 (12, 14, 14) Knit.

Row 13 (13, 15, 15) K3 (1, 3, 3), FR, [K3, FR] to last 3 (1, 3, 3) sts, K3 (1, 3, 3).

Rows 14–16 (14–16, 16–18, 16–18) Knit.

Row 17 (17, 19, 19) K1 (3, 1, 1), FR, [K3, FR] to last 1 (3, 1, 1) sts, K1 (3, 1, 1).

Row 18 (18, 20, 20) Knit.

Rows 19–21 (19–21, 21–23, 21–23) Rep Rows 11–13.

BO knitwise.

FINISHING

Sew side and sleeve seams. Sew on buttons to correspond with buttonholes.

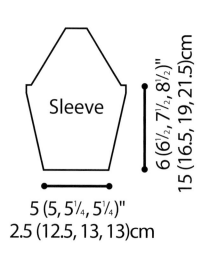

Sleeve

6 (6½, 7½, 8½)"
15 (16.5, 19, 21.5)cm

5 (5, 5¼, 5¼)"
2.5 (12.5, 13, 13)cm

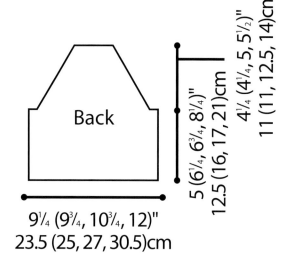

Back

5 (6¼, 6¾, 8¼)"
12.5 (16, 17, 21)cm

4¼ (4¼, 5, 5½)"
11 (11, 12.5, 14)cm

9¼ (9¾, 10¾, 12)"
23.5 (25, 27, 30.5)cm

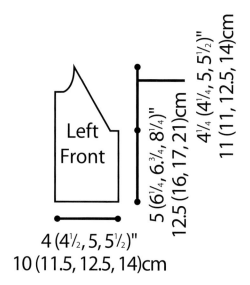

Left
Front

5 (6¼, 6¾, 8¼)"
12.5 (16, 17, 21)cm

4¼ (4¼, 5, 5½)"
11 (11, 12.5, 14)cm

4 (4½, 5, 5½)"
10 (11.5, 12.5, 14)cm

Cabled Vest

Measurements
Skill Level ★ ★ ★

Size	0–6 months	6–12 months	12–18 months	
To Fit Chest	18 46	20 51	22 56	in cm
Actual Size	20 51	22 56	24 61	in cm
Full Length (approximately)	10.5 25.5	11.25 28.5	12.75 32	in cm
Debbie Bliss Baby Cashmerino (Pool 071)	3	3	4	1.75oz/50g; 137yds/125m

Materials

* 1 Pair US 2 (2.75mm) knitting needles
* 1 Pair US 3 (3.25mm) knitting needles OR SIZE TO OBTAIN GAUGE
* Cable needle (cn)
* Stitch markers
* Stitch holders

Gauge

25 sts and 36 rows = 4in/10cm in St st with larger needles. TAKE TIME TO CHECK GAUGE.

SPECIAL ABBREVIATIONS

2/2 Rib (over an even number of sts) **Row 1 (RS)** K2, [P2, K2] across. **Row 2** P2, [K2, P2] across. Rep Rows 1–2.

C4B Sl 2 sts to cn and hold to back of work, K2, K2 from cn.

C4F Sl 2 sts to cn and hold to front of work, K2, K2 from cn.

C4BP Sl 1 st to cn and hold to back of work, K3, P1 from cn.

C4FP Sl 3 sts to cn and hold to front of work, P1, K3 from cn.

C6B Sl 3 sts to cn and hold to back of work, K3, K3 from cn.

C6F Sl 3 sts to cn and hold to front of work, K3, K3 from cn.

BACK

With smaller needles CO 90 (98, 106).

Rows 1–10 (10, 12) 2/2 rib.

Change to larger needles.

Row 11 (11, 13) (RS) K6 (10, 14), pm, work chart, pm, K6 (10, 14).

Row 12 (12, 14) P6 (10, 14), work chart bet markers, P6 (10, 14).

Rows 13–14 (13–, 25–16) K6 (10, 14), work chart bet markers, K6 (10, 14)

The last 4 rows place chart and side sts in St st with G st stripe every 4th row.

Cont as set, working appropriate rows of chart commencing with Row 5 of chart.

Rows 15–54 (15–58, 17–68) Work in patt as established or until back measures 6 (6.5, 7.5)in/15 (16.5, 19)cm from beg, ending with WS row.

Shape Armholes Maintaining patt,

Rows 55–56 (59–60, 69–70) BO 5 sts at beg of row — 80 (88, 96) sts.

Row 57 (61, 71) Dec 1 st at each end of row.

Row 58 (62, 72) Work even.

Rows 59–66 (63–72, 73–82) Rep last 2 rows — 70 (76, 84) sts.

Rows 67–94 (73–100, 83–116) Work even or until armhole measures 4.5 (4.75, 5.25)in/11 (12, 13) cm), ending with WS row.

Shape Shoulders Maintaining patt,

Rows 95–96 (101–102, 117–118) BO 7 (9, 10) sts at beg of row — 56 (58, 64) sts.

Rows 97–98 (103–104, 119–120) BO 8 (9, 11) sts at beg of row — 40 (40, 42) sts.

Place rem 40 (40, 42) sts on holder.

FRONT

Work as for back to Row 78 (82, 96) or 16 (18, 20) rows less than back at start of shoulder shaping, ending with WS row.

Shape Neck Maintaining patt,

Row (RS) 79 (83, 97) Work 22 (25, 28) sts, place center 26 (26, 28) sts onto holder, leave rem 22 (25, 28) sts unworked.

Rows 80–86 (84–90, 98–104) Dec 1 st at neck edge — 15 (18, 21) sts.

Rows 87–94 (91–100, 105–116) Work even.

Shape Shoulder Maintaining patt,

Row 95 (101, 117) BO 7 (9, 10) sts at beg of row — 8 (9, 11) sts.

Row 96 (102, 118) Work even.

Row 97 (103, 119) BO rem 8 (8, 11) sts.

Cable Chart

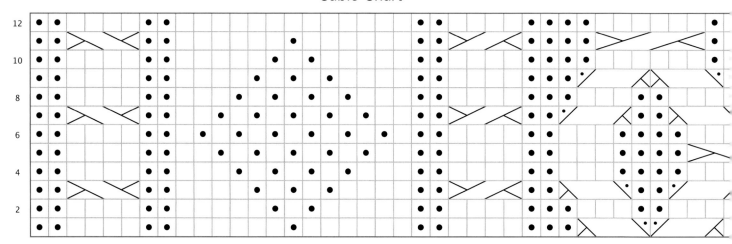

Second Side

With RS facing, join yarn to work rem sts in patt as established — 22 (25, 28) sts.

Complete to match first side, reversing shaping by working an extra row before shoulder shaping.

NECKBAND

Sew right shoulder seam.

With RS facing, using smaller needles, pick up and K14 (18, 20) sts on left side of neck, K26 (26, 28) sts from center front holder, pick up and K14 (18, 20) sts on right side of neck, K40 (40, 42) sts from back holder — 94 (102, 110) sts.

Rows 1–9 (9, 11) 2/2 rib.

Row 10 (10, 12) With larger needles, BO in rib.

ARMHOLE BANDS

Sew left shoulder seam.

With RS facing, using smaller needles, pick and K70 (74, 78) sts evenly around armhole edge.

Rows 1–9 (9, 11) 2/2 rib.

Row 10 (10, 12) With larger needles, BO in rib.

Rep for right armhole.

FINISHING

Sew neckband, side seams and armhole bands. Weave in ends.

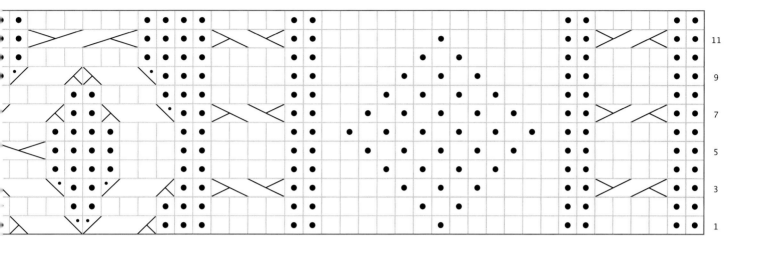

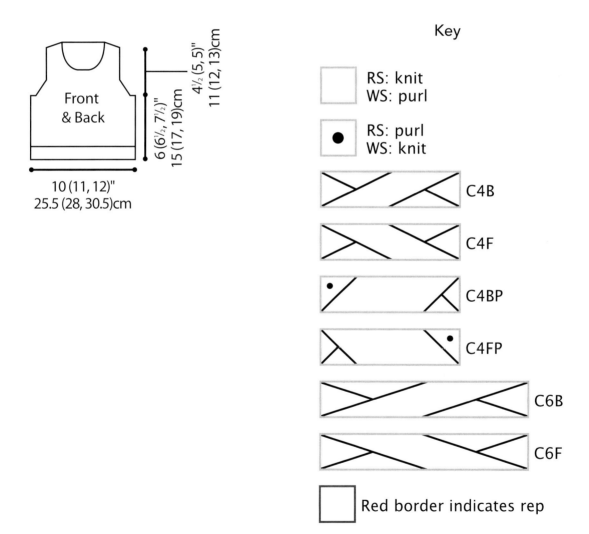

Front & Back

10 (11, 12)"
25.5 (28, 30.5)cm

6 (6½, 7½)"
15 (17, 19)cm

4½ (5, 5)"
11 (12,13)cm

Key

☐	RS: knit WS: purl
●	RS: purl WS: knit

C4B

C4F

C4BP

C4FP

C6B

C6F

☐ Red border indicates rep

Loop Stitch Cardigan

Measurements

Skill Level ★ ★

Size	0–3 months	3–6 months	6–12 months	12–18 months	
To Fit Chest	16 41	18 46	20 51	22 56	in cm
Actual Size	19 48	21 53	22.5 57	24.5 62	in cm
Full Length (approximately)	9.5 24	10.5 26.5	11.5 29	13.5 34	in cm
Sleeve Length (adjustable)	6 15	6.5 16.5	7.5 19	8.5 21.5	in cm
Red Heart Lisa DK (Rose 206)	4	5	5	6	1.75oz/50g; 145yds/133m

Materials

* 1 Pair US 3 (3.25mm) knitting needles
* 1 Pair US 6 (4mm) knitting needles OR SIZE TO OBTAIN GAUGE
* 5 (5, 5, 6) Buttons
* Sewing needle and thread

Gauge

18 sts and 30 rows = 4in (10cm) in ML patt with larger needles. TAKE TIME TO CHECK GAUGE.

SPECIAL ABBREVIATIONS

1/1 Rib (over an odd number of sts) **Row 1** K1, (P1, K1) across. **Row 2** P1, (K1, P1) across. Rep Rows 1–2.

ML K1 keeping st on LH Needle, bring yarn forward bet needles, pass yo left thumb to make a loop, yarn back bet needles and knit st again, sl st off LH Needle, yarn forward and over needle to back, pass 2 sts just worked over loop.

BACK

Ribbing

With smaller needles, CO 55 (59, 63, 67) sts.

Rows 1–9 1/1 Rib.

Row 10 (WS) K2 (4, 6, 8), [K2tog, K3] 10 times, K2tog, K1 (3, 5, 7) — 44 (48, 52, 56) sts.

Body

Row 11 (RS) Change to larger needles, [K1, ML] to last 2 sts, K2.

Row 12 Knit.

Row 13 K2, [ML, K1] across.

Row 14 Knit.

Rep last 4 rows for patt.

Work even in patt as established until back measures 9.5 (10.75, 11.5, 13.5)in/24 (27, 29, 34)cm, ending with WS row. BO.

LEFT FRONT

Ribbing

With smaller needles, CO 25 (27, 29, 31) sts.

Rows 1–9 1/1 Rib.

Row 10 (WS) K2, [K2tog, K3] 4 times, K2tog, K1 (3, 5, 7) — 20 (22, 24, 26) sts.

Body

Row 11 (RS) Change to larger needles, [K1, ML] to last 2 sts, K2.

Row 12 Knit.

Row 13 K2, [ML, K1] across.

Row 4 Knit.

Rep last 4 rows for patt.

Work even in patt as established until measures 7.25 (8.25, 9, 11)in/18 (21, 23, 28)cm, ending with RS row.

Shape Neck Maintaining patt,

Row 1 BO 2 (3, 3, 3) sts, work across — 18 (19, 21, 23) sts.

Rows 2–8 (8, 10, 10) Dec 1 st at neck edge on RS rows 4 (4, 5, 5) times — 14 (15, 16, 18) sts.

Work even until left front measures 9.5 (10.75, 11.5, 13.5)in/24 (27, 29, 34)cm, ending with WS row. BO.

RIGHT FRONT

Ribbing

With smaller needles, CO 25 (27, 29, 31) sts.

Rows 1–9 1/1 Rib.

Row 10 (WS) K2 (4, 6, 8), [K2tog, K3] 4 times, K2tog, K1 — 20 (22, 24, 26) sts.

Body

Row 11 (RS) Change to larger needles, [K1, ML] to last 2 sts, K2.

Row 12 Knit.

Row 13 K2, [ML, K1] across.

Row 14 Knit.

Rep last 4 rows for patt.

Work even in patt until right front measures 7.25 (8.25, 9, 11)in/18 (21, 23, 28)cm, ending with WS row.

Shape Neck Maintaining patt,

Row 1 BO 2 (3, 3, 3) sts, work across — 18 (19, 21, 23) sts.

Rows 2-5 (9, 11, 11) Dec 1 st at neck edge on RS rows 4 (4, 5, 5) times — 14 (15, 16, 18) sts.

Work even until right front measures 9.5 (10.75, 11.5, 13.5)in/24 (27, 29, 34)cm, ending with WS row. BO.

SLEEVES (Make 2)

Ribbing

With smaller needles, CO 31 (31, 33, 33) sts.

Rows 1–9 1/1 Rib.

Row 10 (WS) K15, m1, Knit across — 32 (32, 34, 34) sts.

Arm

Row 11 (RS) Change to larger needles, [K1, ML] to last 2 sts, K2.

Row 12 Knit.

Row 13 K2, [ML, K1] across.

Row 14 Knit.

Rep last 4 rows for patt.

Row 15 Cont in patt, inc 1 st at each end of row 34 (34, 36, 36) sts.

Rows 16–34 (40, 40, 58) Cont in patt, inc 1 st at each end of every 6th row 3 (5, 5, 7) times — 40 (44, 46, 50) sts.

Work even in patt until sleeve measures 6 (6.5, 7.5, 8.5)in/15 (16.5, 19, 21.5)cm, ending with WS row.

Shape Cap Maintaining patt,

BO 5 (5, 6, 6) sts at beg of next 6 rows — 10 (14, 10, 14) sts.

BO rem 10 (14, 10, 14) sts.

NECKBAND

Sew shoulder seams.

Row 1 With RS facing, using smaller needles, pick up and K20 (21, 21, 21) sts evenly along right side of neck, pick up and K16 (18, 20, 20) sts evenly from back of neck and pick up and K20 (21, 21, 21) sts evenly along left side of neck — 56 (60, 62, 62) sts.

Row 2 (WS) Knit, inc 3 sts evenly across row — 59 (63, 65, 65) sts.

Rows 3–8 1/1 Rib. BO in rib.

RIGHT BORDER

Row 1 With RS facing, using smaller needles, pick up and K9 sts evenly along rib, pick up and K36 (40, 48, 58) sts evenly along front edge, pick up and K6 sts evenly along neckband — 51 (55, 63, 73) sts.

Row 2 (WS) Knit.

Rows 3–4 (RS) 1/1 Rib.

Row 5 Buttonhole row Rib 2, [BO 2 sts, rib 9 (10, 12, 11)] 4 (4, 4, 5) times, BO 2 sts, rib 3 (3, 4).

Row 6 Rib 3 (3, 3, 4), CO 2 sts, [rib 9 (10, 12, 11), CO 2 sts] 4 (4, 4, 5) times, rib 2.

Rows 7–8 Rep Rows 3–4. BO in rib.

LEFT BORDER

Row 1 With RS facing, using smaller needles, pick and K6 sts evenly along neckband, pick and K36 (40, 48, 58) sts evenly along front edge and pick and K9 sts evenly along rib — 51 (55, 63, 73) sts.

Row 2 (WS) Knit.

Rows 3–8 1/1 Rib. BO in rib.

FINISHING

Fold sleeves in half lengthwise, and mark center of cap. Match marker to shoulder seam and sew sleeves in place. Sew side and sleeve seams. Sew on buttons to correspond with buttonholes.

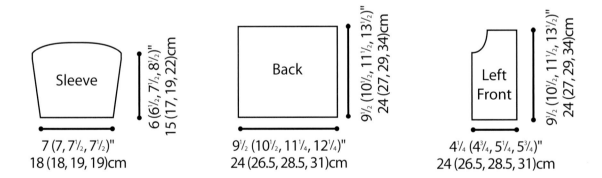

Sleeve

6 (6½, 7½, 8½)"
15 (17, 19, 22)cm

7 (7, 7½, 7½)"
18 (18, 19, 19)cm

Back

9½ (10½, 11½, 13½)"
24 (27, 29, 34)cm

9½ (10½, 11¼, 12¼)"
24 (26.5, 28.5, 31)cm

Left
Front

9½ (10½, 11¼, 13½)"
24 (27, 29, 34)cm

4¼ (4¾, 5¼, 5¾)"
24 (26.5, 28.5, 31)cm

Lace and Seed Stitch Cardigan

Measurements   **Skill Level ★ ★ ★**

Size	0–3 months	3–6 months	6–12 months	12–18 months	
To Fit Chest	16 41	18 46	20 51	22 56	in cm
Actual Size	18 46	20.5 52	22.5 57	25 63.5	in cm
Full Length (approximately)	8.5 22	10 26	12 30	13.5 34	in cm
Sleeve Length (adjustable)	6 15	6.5 16.5	7.5 19	8.5 21.5	in cm
Lion Brand Baby Soft (Baby Pink Pompadour 201)	1	1	2	2	4oz/113g; 459yds/420m

Materials

* 1 Pair US 3 (3.25mm) knitting needles
* 1 Pair US 6 (4mm) knitting needles OR SIZE TO OBTAIN GAUGE
* Stitch holders
* 5 Buttons
* Sewing needle and thread

Gauge

22 sts and 36 rows = 4in/10cm over patt with larger needles. TAKE TIME TO CHECK GAUGE.

SPECIAL ABBREVIATIONS

Seed st (over an odd number of sts) K1, [P1, K1] across. (Knit the purls, purl the knits).

Slip next st from LHN to RHN as if to Knit, without knitting them, K next st, pass slipped st over the K st — 1 st decreased.

Lace Pattern

Row 1 (RS) [K4, yo, skpo] to last 3 sts, K3.

Rows 2, 4, 6 Purl.

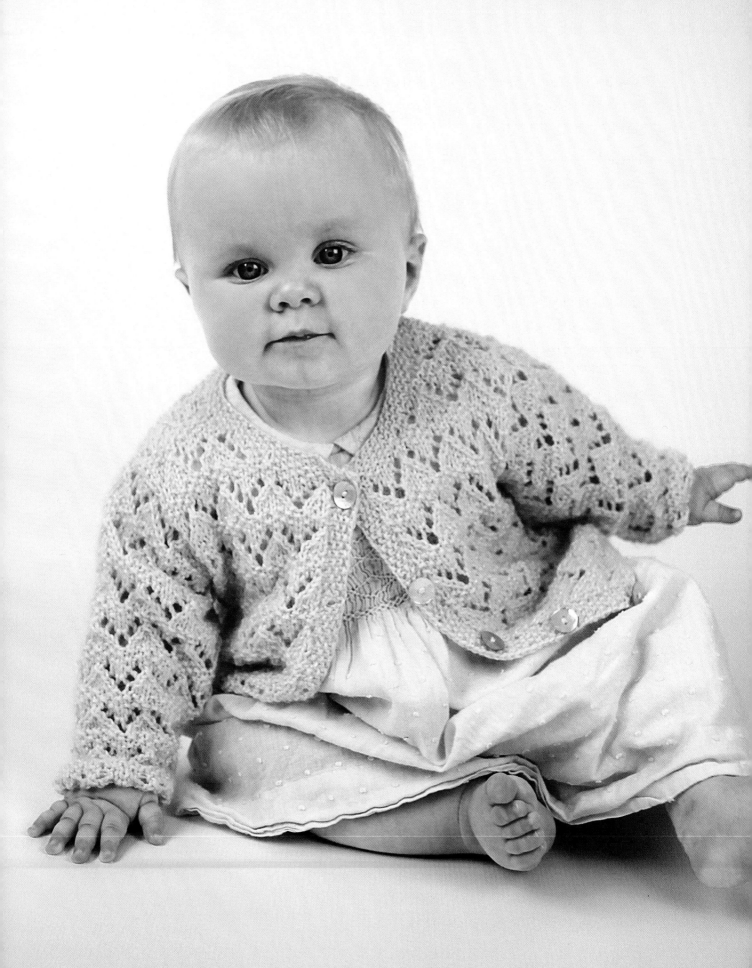

Row 3 K2, [K2tog, yo, K1, yo, skpo, K1] to last st, K1.

Row 5 K1, K2tog, yo, [K3, yo, sl 1, K2tog, psso, yo] to last 6 sts, K3, yo, skpo, K1.

Rows 7–10 K1, [P1, K1] across.

BACK

With smaller needles, CO 51 (57, 63, 69) sts.

Rows 1–4 Seed st.

Change to larger needles, work lace pattern until back measures 4.5 (5.5, 6.75, 8) in/11 (14, 17, 20)cm, ending with WS row.

Shape Armholes Maintaining lace pattern,

BO 3 sts at beg of next 2 rows — 45 (51, 57, 63) sts.

Dec 1 st at each end of next 4 RS rows — 37 (43, 49, 55) sts.

Work even in patt until armhole measures 4.5 (4.75, 5.25, 5.5)in/11 (12, 13, 14)cm, ending with WS row.

Shape Shoulders Maintaining lace pattern,

BO 3 (3, 4, 5) sts at beg of next 4 rows — 25 (31, 33, 35) sts.

BO 2 (4, 4, 4) sts at beg of next 2 rows. Place rem 21 (23, 25, 27) sts on holder.

LEFT FRONT

With smaller needles, CO 27 (29, 33, 35).

Rows 1–4 Seed st.

Change to larger needles, work lace pattern until left front measures 4.5 (5.5, 6.75, 8)in/11 (14, 17, 20)cm, ending with WS row.

Shape Armholes Maintaining lace pattern,

BO 3 sts at beg of next row — 24 (26, 30, 32) sts.

Work even 1 row.

Dec 1 st at armhole edge on next 4 RS rows — 20 (22, 26, 28) sts.

Work even until armhole measures 2.75 (3, 3, 3.5)in/7 (7.5, 7.5, 9)cm or 16 (16, 18, 18) rows less than back at start of shoulder shaping, ending with WS row.

Shape Neck Maintaining lace pattern,

Next row (RS) Work to last 5 (5, 6, 6) sts, turn and place these on a 5 (5, 6, 6) sts holder — 15 (17, 20, 22) sts.

Dec 1 st at neck edge on next 4 rows — 11 (13, 16, 18) sts.

Dec 1 st at neck edge on next 3 (3, 4, 4) RS rows — 8 (10, 12, 14) sts.

Work even 5 rows.

Shape Shoulder Maintaining lace pattern,

BO 3 (3, 4, 5) sts at beg of next 2 RS rows.

Work even 1 row. BO rem 2 (4, 4, 4) sts.

RIGHT FRONT

With smaller needles, CO 27 (29, 33, 35).

Rows 1–4 Seed st.

Change to larger needles, work lace pattern until right front measures 4.5 (5.5, 6.75, 8)in/11 (14, 17, 20)cm, ending with WS row.

Shape Armholes Maintaining lace pattern,

BO 3 sts at beg of next row — 24 (26, 30, 32) sts.

Dec 1 st at armhole edge on next 4 RS rows — 20 (22, 26, 28) sts.

Work even until armhole measures 2.75 (3, 3, 3.5)in/7 (7.5, 7.5, 9)cm or 16 (16, 18, 18) rows less than back at start of shoulder shaping, ending with WS row.

Shape Neck Maintaining lace pattern,

Next row (RS) Work 5 (5, 6, 6) sts, move to holder, work across — 15 (17, 20, 22) sts.

Dec 1 st at neck edge on next 4 rows — 11 (13, 16, 18) sts

Dec 1 st at neck edge on next 3 (3, 4, 4) RS rows — 8 (10, 12, 14) sts.

Work even 6 rows, ending with RS row.

Shape Shoulder Maintaining lace pattern,

BO 3 (3, 4, 5) sts at beg of next 2 WS rows.

Work even 1 row. BO rem 2 (4, 4, 4) sts.

SLEEVES (Make 2)

With smaller needles, CO 27 (29, 33, 35).

Rows 1–4 Seed st.

Change to larger needles.

Row 5 (RS) [K4, yo, skpo] to last 3 (5, 3, 5) sts, K3 (5, 3, 5).

Rows 6, 8, 10 Purl.

Row 7 Kfb into first st, K1, [K2tog, yo, K1, yo, skpo, K1] to last 1 (3, 1, 3) sts, [K2tog, yo] 0 (1, 0, 1) time, Kfb into last st — Inc 2 sts.

Row 9 K2, K2tog, yo, [K3, yo, sl 1, K2tog, psso, yo] to last 7 (3, 7, 3) sts, K3, [yo, skpo, K2] 1 (0, 1, 0) time.

Row 11 Kfb into first st, Seed st to last st, Kfb into last st — Inc 2 sts.

Rows 12–14 Seed st.

Cont in lace pattern as established, inc 1 st at each end of next and every 4th row until there are 47 (51, 55, 59) sts.

Work even in lace pattern until sleeve measures 6 (6.5, 7.5, 8.5)in/15 (16.5, 19, 21.5)cm, ending with WS row.

Shape Cap Maintaining lace pattern,

BO 3 sts at beg of next 2 rows — 41 (45, 49, 53) sts.

Dec 1 st at each end of next 4 RS rows — 33 (37, 41, 45) sts.

Work even 1 row. BO rem 33 (37, 41, 45) sts.

NECK BORDER

Sew shoulder seams.

Row 1 With RS facing, using smaller needles, slip 5 (5, 6, 6) sts from right front st holder to RH needle, join yarn, pick up and K15 (16, 17, 18) sts along right side of neck, K21 (23, 25, 27) sts from back st holder, pick up and K15 (16, 17, 18) sts along left side of neck, Seed st across 5 (5, 6, 6) sts from left front st holder — 61 (65, 71, 75) sts.

Rows 2–6 Seed st. BO in Seed st.

BUTTON BORDER

Row 1 With RS facing, using smaller needles, pick up and K43 (51, 59, 67) sts evenly along left front opening edge, bet top of neck border and CO edge.

Rows 2–6 Seed st. BO in Seed st.

BUTTONHOLE BORDER

Row 1 With RS facing, using smaller needles, pick up and K43 (51, 59, 67) sts evenly along right front opening edge, between CO edge and top of neck border.

Rows 2–3 Seed st.

Row 4 Buttonhole row (WS) Work 2 sts, [dec 1, yo, work 7 (9, 11, 13) sts] to last 5 sts, dec 1, yo, work 3 sts.

Rows 5–6 Seed st. BO in Seed st.

FINISHING

Fold sleeves in half lengthwise and mark center of cap. Match marker to shoulder seam and sew sleeves in place. Sew side and sleeve seams. Sew on buttons to correspond with buttonholes.

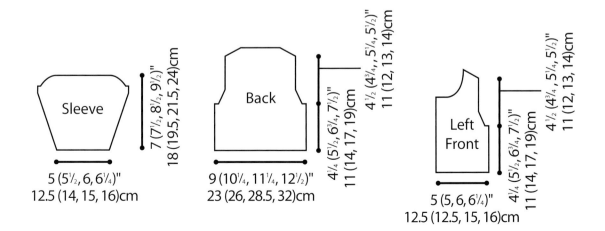

Sleeve

7 (7½, 8½, 9½)"
18 (19.5, 21.5, 24)cm

5 (5½, 6, 6¼)"
12.5 (14, 15, 16)cm

Back

4½ (4¾, 5¼, 5½)"
11 (12, 13, 14)cm

4¼ (5½, 6¾, 7½)"
11 (14, 17, 19)cm

9 (10¼, 11¼, 12½)"
23 (26, 28.5, 32)cm

Left Front

4½ (4¾, 5¼, 5½)"
11 (12, 13, 14)cm

4¼ (5½, 6¾, 7½)"
11 (14, 17, 19)cm

5 (5, 6, 6¼)"
12.5 (12.5, 15, 16)cm

Cabled Cardigan

Measurements

Skill Level ★ ★

Size	0–3 months	3–6 months	6–12 months	12–18 months	
To Fit Chest	16 41	18 46	20 51	22 56	in cm
Actual Size	20 51	22.5 56	24 61	25.5 65	in cm
Full Length (approximately)	11 28	12 30.5	13 33	15 38	in cm
Sleeve Length (adjustable)	6 15	6.5 16.5	7.5 19	8.5 21.5	in cm
Cascade 220 Superwash Aran (Feather Grey 875)	2	3	3	4	3.5oz/100g; 150yds;177.5m

Materials

* 1 Pair US 6 (4mm) knitting needles
* 1 Pair US 8 (5mm) knitting needles OR SIZE TO OBTAIN GAUGE
* 1 US 6 (4mm) 32in/80cm circular needle
* Stitch markers
* Stitch holder
* Cable needle (cn)
* 3 (3, 4, 4) Buttons
* Sewing needle and thread

Gauge

18 sts and 24 rows = 4in/10cm in St st with larger needles. TAKE TIME TO CHECK GAUGE.

SPECIAL ABBREVIATIONS

2/2 Rib (over an even number of sts) **Row 1 (RS)** K2, [P2, K2] across. **Row 2** P2, [K2, P2] across. Rep Row 1–2.

Kfb on K rows and Pfb on P rows.

T2B Slip next st to cn and hold to back of work, K1, P1 from cn.

T2F Slip next st to cn and hold to front of work, P1, K1 from cn.

C6B Slip next 3 sts to cn and hold to back of work, K3, K3 from cn.

C6F Slip next 3 sts to cn and hold to front of work, K3, K3 from cn.

BACK

With smaller needles, CO 46 (50, 54, 58).

Rows 1–8 2/2 Rib

Change to larger needles and set up for cable charts as foll:

Row 9 (RS) K2, P2, pm, beg chart A over next 14 sts, pm, P2, K6 (10, 14, 18), P2, pm, beg chart B over next 14 sts, pm, P2, K2.

Row 10 P2, K2, work row 2 of chart B bet markers, K2, P6 (10, 14, 18), K2, work row 2 of chart A bet markers, K2, P2.

Rows 11–64 (70, 74, 88) Work even, maintaining patt as established.

Shape shoulders Maintaining patt as established,

Rows 65–66 (71–72, 75–76, 89–90) BO 8 (9, 9, 10) sts at beg of row — 30 (32, 36, 38) sts.

Rows 67–68 (73–74, 77–78, 91–92) BO 7 (8, 9, 10) sts at beg of rows — 16 (16, 18, 18) sts.

Place rem 16 (16, 18, 18) sts on holder.

LEFT FRONT

With smaller needles, CO 22 (24, 26, 28).

Rows 1–8 2/2 Rib.

Change to larger needles and set up for cable charts as foll:

Row 9 (RS) K2, P2, pm, beg chart A over next 14 sts, pm, P2, K2 (4, 6, 8).

Row 10 P2 (4, 6, 8), K2, work row 2 of chart A bet markers, K2, P2.

Rows 11–36 (42, 44, 54) Work even, maintaining patt as established.

Shape neck Maintaining patt as established,

Dec 1 st at end (front edge) of next row — 21 (23, 25, 27) sts.

Dec 1 st at end of every 4th row 6 (6, 7, 7) times — 15 (17, 18, 20) sts.

Work 3 (3, 1, 5) rows even, ending with WS row.

Shape shoulder Maintaining patt as established,

BO 8 (9, 9, 10) sts at beg of next row.

BO 7 (8, 9, 10) sts at beg of foll alt row.

RIGHT FRONT

With smaller needles, CO 22 (24, 26, 28).

Row 1 (RS) P0 (2, 0, 2), K2, 2/2 rib across.

Rows 2–8 2/2 Rib.

Change to larger needles and set up for cable charts as foll:

Row 9 (RS) K2 (4, 6, 8), P2, pm, beg chart B over next 14 sts, pm, P2, K2.

Row 10 P2, K2, work row 2 of chart B bet markers, K2, P2 (4, 6, 8).

Rows 11–36 (42, 44, 54) Work even, maintaining patt as established.

Shape neck Maintaining patt as established,

Dec 1 st at beg (front edge) of next row — 21 (23, 25, 27) sts.

Dec 1 st at beg of every 4th row 6 (6, 7, 7) times — 15 (17, 18, 20) sts.

Work 4 (4, 2, 6) rows even, ending with RS row.

Shape shoulder Maintaining patt as established,

BO 8 (9, 9, 10) sts at beg of next row.

BO 7 (8, 9, 10) sts at beg of foll alt row.

LEFT SLEEVE

With smaller needles, CO 22 (22, 26, 26).

Row 1 (RS) P0 (0, 2, 2), K2, 2/2 Rib to last 0 (0, 2, 2) sts, P0 (0, 2, 2).

Rows 2–8 2/2 Rib.

Change to larger needles and set up for cable charts as foll:

Row 9 (RS) K2 (2, 4, 4), P2, pm, beg chart A over next 14 sts, pm, P2, K2 (2, 4, 4).

Row 10 P2 (2, 4, 4), K2, work row 2 of chart A bet markers, K2, P2 (2, 4, 4).

Shape Sleeve Maintaining patt as established,

Inc 1 st at each end of next row — 24 (24, 28, 28) sts.

Inc 1 st at each end of every 3rd row 8 (8, 9, 11) times — 40 (40, 46, 50) sts.

Work even until sleeve measures 6 (6.5, 7.5, 8.5)in/15 (16.5. 19, 21.5)cm, ending with WS row.

Shape Cap Maintaining patt as established,

BO 5 (5, 6, 6) sts at beg of next 6 rows — 10 (10, 10, 14) sts.

BO rem 10 (10, 10, 14) sts.

RIGHT SLEEVE

Work as for left sleeve, using chart B instead of chart A.

BORDER

Sew shoulder seams.

Row 1 (RS) With circular needle, starting at lower front, pick up and K23 (27, 31,

37) sts evenly along straight edge, pick up and K20 (20, 23, 25) sts evenly along shaped edge, K16 (16, 18, 18) sts from holder, pick up and K20 (20, 23, 25) sts evenly along shaped edge, pick up and K23 (27, 31, 37) sts evenly along straight edge — 102 (110, 126, 142) sts.

Rows 2–3 G st.

FOR GIRL

Row 4 Buttonhole row (WS) K to last 21 (25, 29, 35) sts, yo, K2tog, [K6 (8, 6, 8), yo, K2tog] 2 (2, 3, 3) times, K3.

FOR BOY

Row 4 Buttonhole row (WS) K3, K2tog, yo, [K6 (8, 6, 8), K2tog, yo] 2 (2, 3, 3) times, K to end.

ALL VERSIONS

Rows 5–6 G st.

BO knitwise.

FINISHING

Fold sleeves in half lengthwise, mark center of cap. Match marker to shoulder seam and sew sleeves in place. Sew side and sleeve seams. Sew on buttons to correspond with buttonholes.

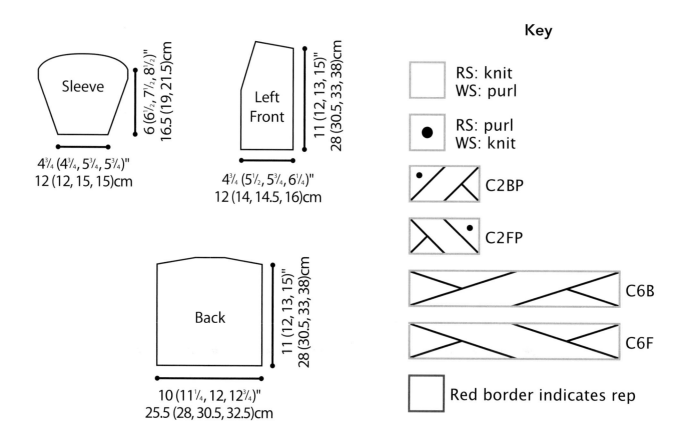

Sleeve

6 (6½, 7½, 8½)"
16.5 (19, 21.5)cm

4¾ (4¾, 5¾, 5¾)"
12 (12, 15, 15)cm

Left Front

11 (12, 13, 15)"
28 (30.5, 33, 38)cm

4¾ (5½, 5¾, 6¼)"
12 (14, 14.5, 16)cm

Back

11 (12, 13, 15)"
28 (30.5, 33, 38)cm

10 (11¼, 12, 12¾)"
25.5 (28, 30.5, 32.5)cm

Key

□	RS: knit / WS: purl
▣	RS: purl / WS: knit
	C2BP
	C2FP
	C6B
	C6F
□	Red border indicates rep

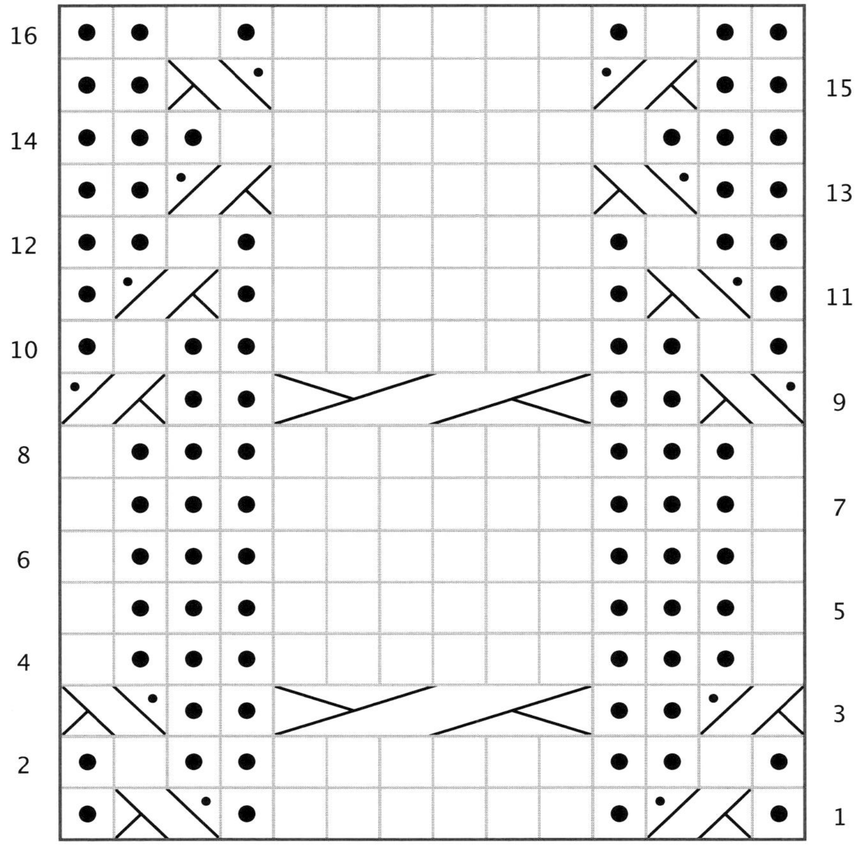

Chart B

15 13 11 9 7 5 3 1

16 14 12 10 8 6 4 2

Chart A

15 13 11 9 7 5 3 1

16 14 12 10 8 6 4 2

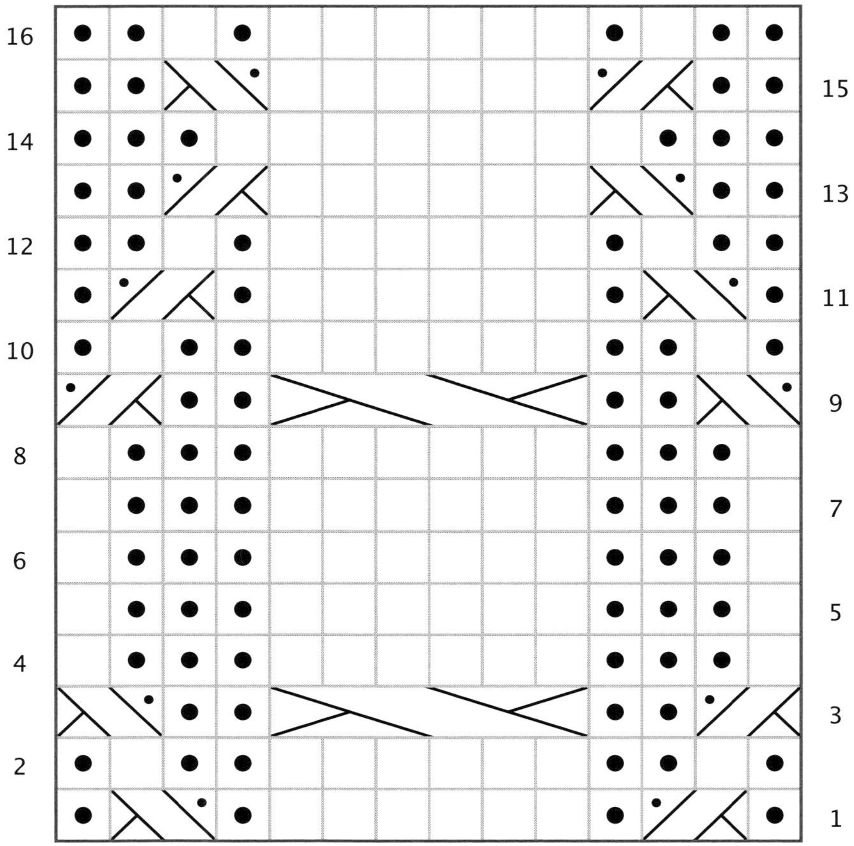

Cabled Pullover

Measurements

Size	0–6 months	6–12 months	12–18 months	
To Fit Chest	18 46	20 51	22 56	in cm
Actual Size	21 53	22.5 57	24 61	in cm
Full Length (approximately)	10.5 27	11.5 29	13.5 34	in cm
Sleeve Length (adjustable)	6.5 16.5	7.5 19	8.5 21.5	in cm
Cascade 220 Superwash Aran (Strawberry Cream 894)	3	3	4	3.5oz/50g; 150yds/137.5m

Materials

* 1 Pair US 6 (4mm) knitting needles
* 1 Pair US 8 (5mm) knitting needles OR SIZE TO OBTAIN GAUGE
* Stich holders
* Stitch markers
* Cable needle (cn)

Gauge

19 sts and 26 rows = (4in/10cm) in Double Seed st with larger needles.

SPECIAL ABBREVIATIONS

2/2 Rib (over an even number of sts) **Row 1 (RS)** K2, [P2, K2] across. **Row 2** P2, [K2, P2] across. Rep Rows 1–2.

Rib Knit or purl sts as indicated to maintain pattern.

TW2B K into front of 2nd st on LH needle without slipping st off needle, K into front of 1st st on LH needle, slipping both sts off needle together.

TW2F K into back of 2nd st on LH needle without slipping st off needle, K into front of 1st st on LH needle, slipping both sts off needle together.

C3BP Slip next st to cn and hold to back of work, K2, P1 from cn.

C3FP Slip next 2 sts to cn and hold to front of work, P1, K2 from cn.

C4B Slip next 2 sts to cn and hold to back of work, K2, K2 from cn.

C4F Slip next 2 sts to cn and hold to front of work, K2, K2 from cn.

C5BP Slip next 3 sts to cn and hold to back of work, K2, slip P st from cn to LH needle, P this st, K2 from cn.

MB (Make Bobble) (Kfbf) into next st, turn. P3, turn. K3, turn. P1, P2tog, turn, K2tog.

Double Seed st (over an odd number of sts) **Rows 1, 4** P1, [K1, P1] across. **Rows 2, 3** K1, [P1, K1] across.

BACK

With smaller needles, CO 50 (54, 58) sts.

Rows 1–7 2/2 Rib.

Row 8 (WS) 2/2 rib, inc 1 st at center of row — 51 (55, 59) sts.

Change to larger needles, work even in Double Seed st until back measures 8 (9, 11)in/20 (23, 28)cm, ending with WS row.

Shape First Side of Neck Maintaining Double Seed st,

Row 1 (RS) Work 22 (23, 25) sts, turn, leaving rem sts unworked.

**Rows 2–6 Dec 1 st at neck edge — 17 (18, 20) sts.

Work even until back measures 10.5 (11.5, 13.5)in/26.5 (29, 34)cm, ending with WS row. BO. **

Shape Second Side of Neck Maintaining Double Seed st,

Row 1 (RS) With RS facing, place 7 (9, 9) sts on holder. Join yarn, work 22 (23, 25) sts.

Work from ** to ** as given for first side of neck.

FRONT

With Smaller needles, CO 50 (54, 58).

Rows 1–7 2/2 Rib.

Row 8 (WS) Rib 7 (9, 11), m1, [rib 1, m1, rib 2, m1] 12 times, rib 7 (9, 11) — 75 (79, 83) sts.

Row 9 Change to larger needles, [P1, K1] 2 (3, 4) times, P2, pm, work row 1 of chart over next 63 sts, pm, P2, [K1, P1] 2 (3, 4) times.

Row 10 Cont Double Seed st over 6 (8, 10) sts, work chart bet markers, Cont Double Seed st over 6 (8, 10) sts.

Work even in patt until front measures 8 (9, 11)in/20 (23, 28)cm, ending with WS row.

Shape First Side of Neck Maintaining patt as established,

Row 1 Work 32 (32, 34) sts, turn, leaving rem sts unworked.

***Rows 2–8** Dec 1 st at neck edge — 25 (25, 27) sts.

Work even until front is 1 row less than back, ending with RS row. ***

Next row (WS) Work 1, [dec 1, work 1] 0 (1, 1) times, [dec 1 st 2 times, work 1] 4 (3, 3) times, work 4 (6, 8) — 17 (18, 20) sts. BO all rem sts.

Shape Second Side of Neck Maintaining patt as established,

Row 1 With RS facing, place 11 (15, 15) sts on holder. Join yarn, work 32 (32, 34) sts.

Work from *** to *** as given for first side of neck.

Next row (WS) Work 5 (7, 9), [dec 1 st 2 times, work 1] 4 (3, 3) times, [dec 1, work 1] 0 (1, 1) times — 17 (18, 20) sts. BO all rem sts.

SLEEVES (Make 2)

With Smaller needles, CO 26 (30, 30).

Rows 1–7 2/2 Rib.

Row 8 (WS) Rib 3, m1, [rib 5 (6, 4), m1] 4 (4, 6) times, rib 3 – 31 (35, 37) sts.

Row 9 Change to larger needles, beg Double Seed st, inc 1 st at each end of row — 33 (37, 39) sts.

Rows 10–29 (33, 34) Maintaining Double Seed st, inc 1 st at each end of every 5th (6th, 5th) row 4 (4, 5) times — 41 (45, 49) sts.

Work even in Double Seed st until sleeve measures 6.5 (7.5, 8.5)in/16.5 (19, 21.5) cm, ending with WS row.

Shape Cap Maintaining patt as established,

BO 5 sts at beg of next 6 rows — 11 (15, 19) sts.

BO rem 11 (15, 19) sts.

NECKBAND

Sew right shoulder seam.

Row 1 (RS) With RS facing, using smaller needles, pick up and K16 sts along left side of front neck, working from holder K1 (0, 0), [K2tog 2 times, K1] 2 (3, 3) times, pick up and K16 sts along right side of front neck, pick up and K16 sts along right side of back neck, work 7 (9, 9) sts from holder at back of neck and pick up and K16 sts along left side of back neck — 78 (82, 82) sts.

Rows 2–8 2/2 Rib.

Rows 9–12 St st. BO loosely.

FINISHING

Sew right shoulder. Reverse seam on neckband and sew closed. Fold sleeves in half lengthwise and mark center of cap. Match sleeve cap marker to shoulder seam. Sew side and sleeve seams.

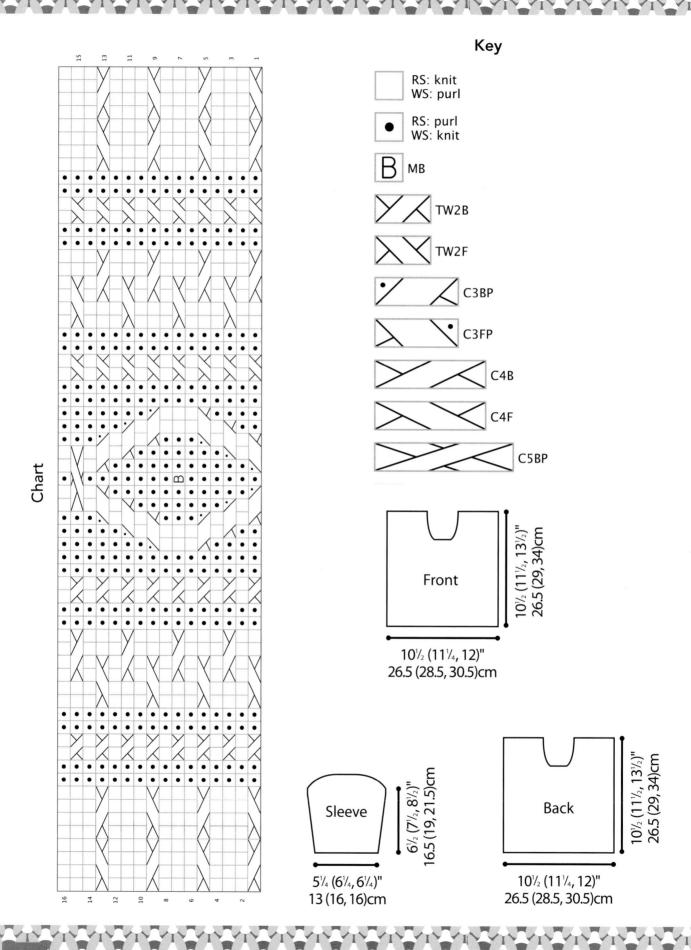

Chart

Key

☐	RS: knit WS: purl
●	RS: purl WS: knit
B	MB
TW2B symbol	TW2B
TW2F symbol	TW2F
C3BP symbol	C3BP
C3FP symbol	C3FP
C4B symbol	C4B
C4F symbol	C4F
C5BP symbol	C5BP

Front

10½ (11½, 13½)"
26.5 (29, 34)cm

10½ (11¼, 12)"
26.5 (28.5, 30.5)cm

Sleeve

6½ (7½, 8½)"
16.5 (19, 21.5)cm

5¼ (6¼, 6¼)"
13 (16, 16)cm

Back

10½ (11½, 13½)"
26.5 (29, 34)cm

10½ (11¼, 12)"
26.5 (28.5, 30.5)cm

Lace and Seed Stitch Dress

Measurements   Skill Level ★ ★ ★

Size	0–3 months	3–6 months	6–12 months	12–18 months	
To Fit Chest	16 41	18 46	20 51	22 56	in cm
Actual Size	18 46	20 51	22 56	24 61	in cm
Full Length (approximately)	14 35.5	15 38	15.5 39	16.5 42	in cm
Sleeve Length (adjustable)	6 15	6.5 16.5	7.5 19	8.5 21.5	in cm
Sirdar Snuggly DK (Petal Pink 212)	5	5	6	7	1.75oz/50g; 179yds/164m

Materials

* 1 Pair US 3 (3.25mm) knitting needles
* 1 Pair US 6 (4mm) knitting needles OR SIZE TO OBTAIN GAUGE
* 1 US 3 (3.25mm) 32in/80cm circular needle
* 1 US 6 (4mm) 32in/80cm circular needle
* Stitch holders
* 3 Buttons
* Sewing needle and thread

Gauge

22 sts and 36 rows = 4in/(10cm) in Seed st with larger needles. TAKE TIME TO CHECK GAUGE.

SPECIAL ABBREVIATIONS

Seed st (over an odd number of sts) K1, (P1, K1) across. (Knit the purls, purl the knits).

S2kpo Slip next 2 sts from LH needle to RH needle as if to K2tog, without knitting them, K next st, pass 2 slipped sts over K st — 2 sts decreased.

BACK

With smaller circular needle, CO 145 (161, 181, 201).

Rows 1–4 Seed st.

Row 5 (RS) Change to larger circular needle, [K1, P1] 0 (1, 0, 2) times, pm, work Row 1 of chart] to last 0 (2, 0, 4) sts, [P1, K1] 0, (1, 0, 2) times. sts, [P1, K1] 0 (1, 0, 2).

Row 6 [K1, P1] 0 (1, 0, 2) times, work chart bet markers (P1, K1) 0 (1, 0, 2).

Rows 7–64 Cont in pattern as established, working chart 2 times.

Rep last 2 rows until back measures 10 (11, 11, 11.5)in/25.5 (28, 28, 29)cm, ending with WS row.

Decrease For Bodice

Next row (RS) K0 (1, 0, 0), K3tog 48 (53, 60, 67) times, K1 (1, 1, 0) — 49 (55, 61, 67) sts.

Work 3 rows G st. **

Work 16 (18, 20, 26) rows in Seed st, ending with WS row.

Divide For Back Opening

First Side

Next row Seed st 22 (25, 28, 31) sts, K5, turn, leaving rem sts unworked.

Next row (RS) K5, Seed st 22 (25, 28, 31).

Buttonhole row Seed st 22 (25, 28, 31), K1, K2tog, yo, K2.

Maintaining Seed st and G st border, work 17 rows, making buttonhole on 10th row, ending with WS row.

Shape Shoulders and Back Neck

Next row BO 15 (18, 19, 22) sts, Seed st to last 5 sts, K5.

Place rem 12 (12, 14, 14) sts on holder.

Second Side

With RS facing, join yarn CO 5 sts, work 22 (25, 28, 31) in Seed st — 27 (30, 33, 36) sts.

Next row (RS) Seed st 22 (25, 28, 31) sts, K5.

Maintaining Seed st and G st border, work 18 rows.

Shape Shoulder and Back Neck

Next row K5, Seed st 7 (7, 9, 9) sts, BO 15 (18, 19, 22) sts.

Place rem 12 (12, 14, 14) sts on holder.

FRONT

Work as given for back to **.

Work 14 (16, 18, 24) rows in Seed st, ending with WS row.

Shape Neck
First Side

Next row Seed st 20 (23, 24, 27) sts, turn, leaving rem sts unworked.

*** **Next row** Work even.

Work 9 rows, dec 1 st at neck edge on RS rows — 15 (18, 19, 22) sts. ***

Work even 11 rows in Seed st, BO.

Second Side

With RS facing, slip 9 (9, 13, 13) sts to holder, join yarn, Seed st across — 20 (23, 24, 27) sts.

Rep from *** to ***.

Work even 11 rows in Seed st, BO.

SLEEVES (Make 2)

With smaller needles, CO 31 (33, 35, 37).

Rows 1–6 Seed st.

Change to larger needles, cont in Seed st, inc 1 st at each end of 3rd row — 33 (35, 37, 39) sts.

Inc 1 st at each end of 6th row 6 (6, 7, 8) times — 45 (47, 51, 55) sts.

Work even in Seed st until sleeve measures 6 (6.5, 7.5, 8.5)in/15 (16.5, 19, 21.5)cm, ending with WS row.

Shape Cap

Maintaining Seed st, BO 5 (5, 6, 6) sts at beg of next 6 rows.

BO rem 15 (17, 15, 19) sts.

NECKBAND

Sew shoulder seams.

With RS facing, using smaller needles, K12 (12, 14, 14) sts from holder at left side of back neck, pick up and K14 sts evenly along left side of front neck, K9 (9, 13, 13) sts from holder at front of neck, pick up and K14 sts evenly along right side of front neck and K12 (12, 14, 14) sts from holder at right side of back neck — 61 (61, 69, 69) sts.

Next row Knit.

Chart

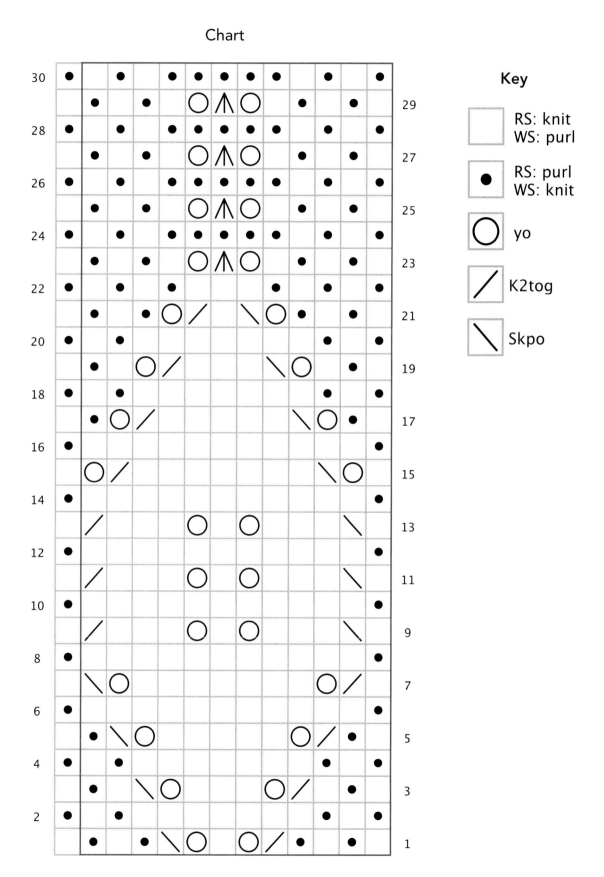

Key

☐	RS: knit WS: purl
●	RS: purl WS: knit
◯	yo
╱	K2tog
╲	Skpo

Buttonhole row (RS) K to last 4 sts, K2tog, yo, K2.

Work 4 rows G st, BO knitwise.

FINISHING

Fold sleeves in half lengthwise and mark center of cap. Match marker to shoulder seam and sew sleeves in place. Sew side and sleeve seams. Sew on buttons to correspond with buttonholes.

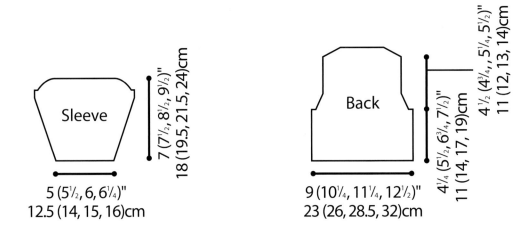

Sleeve

7 (7½, 8½, 9½)"
18 (19.5, 21.5, 24)cm

5 (5½, 6, 6¼)"
12.5 (14, 15, 16)cm

Back

4½ (4¾,, 5¼, 5½)"
11 (12, 13, 14)cm

4¼ (5½, 6¾, 7½)"
11 (14, 17, 19)cm

9 (10¼, 11¼, 12½)"
23 (26, 28.5, 32)cm

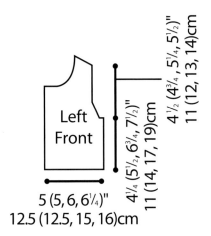

Left
Front

4½ (4¾, 5¼, 5½)"
11 (12, 13, 14)cm

4¼ (5½, 6¾, 7½)"
11 (14, 17, 19)cm

5 (5, 6, 6¼)"
12.5 (12.5, 15, 16)cm

ACKNOWLEDGMENTS

I would like to say a big thank you to all the following people who made this book come to life: Vanessa Putt for commissioning this book and everyone else at Dover Publications for making this book happen; Kim Kotary for editing all the patterns; Mini-Me-Photography, Portsmouth, UK, for her amazing photography. And to the fabulous models, Albie, Brianna, Darcie, Olivia, Ralph, and Tristan; and to their mums for allowing them to model for this book.

YARN SUPPLIERS

USA
Love Knitting
www.loveknitting.com
Tel: 1-866-677-0057
info@loveknitting.com

WEBS
www.yarn.com
Tel: 1-800-367-9327
customerservice@yarn.com

UK
Hobbycraft
www.hobbycraft.co.uk
Tel: +44 (0) 330-026-1400
customerservices@hobbycraft.co.uk

Wool Warehouse
www.woolwarehouse.co.uk
Tel: +44 (0) 192-688-2818
sales@woolwarehouse.co.uk

ABOUT THE AUTHOR

Jody Long was born in Portsmouth, England, in 1984. He grew up in nearby Waterlooville, Hampshire, and in 2014 moved to Málaga, Spain. For over twelve years he designed for all the major UK and US knitting magazines, and then moved on to design for knitting mills around the globe. Jody has also designed for celebrity clients. His own yarn, called "Easy Care Worsted," is available in 30 colors.

Visit Jody's website: www.jodylongknits.com.